OF JOY
AND
SORROW

BETH WISNER JAHNSEN

Of Joy and Sorrow
© 2018 by Beth Wisner Jahnsen
Printed in the United States of America
All rights reserved. This book or any portions thereof may not be reproduced or used in any manner whatsoever without the express written permission of the author except for the use of brief quotations in a book review. For permission requests, write to the author, at "Attention: Permissions Coordinator," at the address below:

P.O. Box 9286
Cedarpines Park, CA 92322

Paperbacks and eBooks available on: Amazon.com
Paperbacks and bulk copies available at: Bethjahnsen.com

Bible verses: New Heart English Bible

ISBN: 9781730896453

Cover Photo by Sharon Wisner
Cover by Miles Jahnsen & Tasha Waldorf
Author photo by David Cervantes

Edited by Janae Lee Ann Tullo

For Janae
Joy is yours, and it will come again.

CONTENTS

FORWARD

OF JOY AND SORROW
   An Introduction   1

HALFWAY TO HEAVEN   7

FALLING INTO FAITH   17

ART   23

I WONDER...   33

MAGIC ROCKS   39

BEING JONAH   45

MILES AND MILES   69

A BEAUTIFUL MIND   75

DAWNS L.A. DAY   83

BLUE JAYS, BULLIES
         AND THE BRAVE   87

FILLING THE GAP   95

THE LIFE OF A HATCHET   109

CALL ME ISAAC   121

GOD'S GRAVITY	129
SILVER AND GOLD	131
MOTHERING THE FATHERLESS	137
THIS LITTLE LIGHT OF MINE	143
LONG WALKS AND COLD SHOWERS	147
YOU CAN'T DRIVE THROUGH ZION AFTER DARK	153
BE THE GOOD	163
GRAPES OF DROUGHT	171
BITTERSWEET REFRAIN	183
EARN THIS	193
THIS STORM OF LIFE	199
PERSPECTIVE	213
CHOOSE HOPE	219
EPILOUGE	223
ABOUT THE AUTHOR	

Acknowledgments
In Order of Appearance

To my mom and dad, **Sharon and Dale Wisner** – Obviously you were there and you know. You know the easy, the hard and the complete and total adventure our lives have been. Thank you for always listening and for always pointing me back towards God. Thank you for teaching me from the earliest of ages what order my priorities should be in. Thank you for catching me when I fell, and for letting me stand back up on my own two feet.

Dawn Johnson – Dearest of sisters, how many times have we laughed so hard we cried and you peed? How many times have we talked each other down, and up? Over the years we have become best friends, business partners, counselors, ATM's, protectors and pretty much everything one can imagine being for another. Thank you for being the other end of my teeter-totter.

Jim Wisner – Thank you for not succeeding in killing me when we were little, I'm sorry for all the bumps, breaks and bleeding you experienced with me standing right next to you. But I think most of the time I was in fact trying to talk you out of whatever was about to hurt you. Thanks for inviting me and my boys to crash in your house and for being chill when we fill up the sink with dirty dishes. We're going to do them tomorrow I promise.

Janae Tullo – Thank you for being a mirror. I was there when you came into this world, and feel privileged to have watched you be born more than once. I am watching again, and I feel lucky to see how strong you are, even in your complete weakness. For your honesty and for editing this book with skill, forthrightness and love, I cannot thank you enough. You have made me a better writer. I can't wait to read your first book.

Chris Johnson – From the sweet two-year-old who talked my ear off, to the eight-year-old who so annoyed his sister, to the suddenly interesting teenager playing guitar and learning everything he could about everything he could, to the adult who is compassionate and someone I know I can always count on no matter what. I love you and thank you for always being there for me and my boys.

My Boys - Oh boy! You are the purpose of my life. You are the realization of the dream I dreamt when I was just five-years-old.

Miles – Thanks for being my concert buddy, my encourager and my friend. Your compassion and tender heart leave me in awe. Watching you take care of those around you fills my heart with joy and pride. For reminding me to write and for making sure I have my keys before I leave the house I thank you. Your tender heart is a gift from God. I am so proud of the man you have become.

Devin – You are the funniest human being I know. Your wit and charm would make me want to know you even if I wasn't your mom. Your incredible knowledge and mind full of facts amaze me daily. One of these days I am going to find something you don't already know about. I know you can change the world for the better, and I LOVE that that is so important to you. I pray your tender heart, the one you try to ignore, never betrays you.

Cole – My sweet, sweet Cole. You are a reminder every single day that God gives us the desires of our hearts. I never imagined that I would be so blessed as to have the kindest, sweetest child on the planet, who is constantly looking at others to make sure they are okay. Thanks for the morning icepacks and the water.

Jerry Wilson - for reminding me that I am a writer.

Tasha Waldorf and ***Wesley Heuler*** for the technical help.

The friends who are so dear to me: Van, Sonja, Kaylee and Karlee Metschke; Chris, Benilda, Nick, Danielle and Alex Duke; Tom Lenton, Stephen, Lindsay and Phoenix Crumbacher, Tammy Renich, my prayer warrior Toni Worlitz, Debi Wilson,

Cathleen Bice, Shawna Diagle, Kurt and Renee Johnson, David Cervantes, Derri Daugherty.

For those who offered me quiet places of retreat to write I thank: Catherine Nixon Hendrickson; Wes Johnson; Joann, Doug, Dallas, Madison and Sierra Leeper; Wes and Heidi Wasson.

When the acknowledgments page seems like the hardest thing to write in your first book, it may very well mean you have too many people to thank, and you don't want to miss anyone, but you also want to keep it short so people will actually read it. If I didn't mention you, and I should have, know that I have incredible appreciation for all my family, friends and readers who have encouraged me to keep writing, have helped me in so many ways and who have been a part of the journey of my life so far. Also know that I am now fifty, and my brain doesn't work as well as it used to. Maybe I'll remember to thank you in my next book – but you'll have to buy it to find out if I did.

FORWARD

AIR
By Janae Lee Ann Tullo

I swear there's something that shifts in the air when life changing events happen. It is almost like the situation demands a universal pause. Much bigger than the emotions we are feeling, and the things going on inside our head. I have always found it fascinating. Falling in love, giving birth to my daughter and experiencing a death are only a few examples of when I've felt it. More recently, the slow and traumatic reveal of an affair that blew the lid off of my life. This air I'm breathing right now is the heaviest kind, raw, seeping with tragedy and betrayal.

My first experience with real heartbreak was watching my aunt lose her husband. It wasn't as sudden as most people from the outside would think. For me, it was like watching a candle burn, tragically slow. The fire remained for her, even through the deepest heartbreaks and setbacks. In many ways when she talks about who he was and the idea she had of him you can still catch a glimpse of the faint glow. Watching this process impacted me more than she will ever know. Planting seeds of hope to help me overcome the little deaths I would be forced to face in my own life. A completely broken woman who has been dragged thru the dirt and somehow gets up every single time to brush herself off. You see, for me it is easy to succumb to the all-encompassing and heaviest type of air that most would define as depression. I couldn't tell you that I would be writing this today if she hadn't gone before me.

I firmly believe that it is through honest and open accounts of heartbreak and defeat that we can find the most comfort. To understand that we are not the first to brave these waters of healing and becoming whole. This collection of essays and short stories paint a beautiful picture of a woman torn apart by the hell that is life on earth only to stand up and say, "We must keep going."

I can only imagine how daunting of a task it must be to write a book. Especially when multiple people in your life have spoken it out and almost expect it from you. I admire Beth's courage to press on with her writing. I hope to someday call upon her for help to do the same. Her writing is encouraging and open. I continue to stand in awe of her courageous spirit. I am proud to be in her family and proud of the hard work she's done to get to this point.

If you are experiencing the air of joy, savor every single sticky sweet drop. If you are experiencing the air of sorrow, try your hardest to lean into the raw, transformative energy. It can be so easy to run from these places because they are scary. They call us to be vulnerable. To step out of our comfort zones and change for the better. It's a journey that I am on right now and I would be lying if I said I was loving the process. Grab onto those who have gone before you. Take courage from their stories. Above all else, be kind to yourself and just keep breathing.

OF JOY AND SORROW
An Introduction

I believe at our creation God has a path for each of us, that if followed would bring us complete joy and contentment. I also believe that there has never been a human being to walk this earth who has not deviated from that path. The miraculous beauty of God's grace is that no matter how far off the path we go, no matter how many times we stray from it, He will lead us to a new and still blessed road with the simple prayer of "Father."

As a parent it's easy to understand His desire for our joy, but it also makes it easy to understand why we still suffer. When my children are in pain I want nothing more than to take that pain from them, which is exactly what Christ death offered us isn't it? And yet we still suffer. I allow my children the continued pain sometimes, because it is part of the joy, the learning of it. The depths of our sorrow will someday be replaced with more joy than we can imagine, I truly believe that.

We are temporal beings and God is not. That is something I will never be able to wrap my brain around completely but trying to understand it is the only way for me to get through this life sometimes. I know the suffering will pass, that things will get better, but it is the time it actually takes walking through the pain that seems too much for me. I wish I could fast forward through all the bad, but that would leave the good without substance, without merit. Joy would be hollow without the experience of pain.

"Count it all joy." "All things work together for good." In the midst of pain and suffering those promises may appear to be just words and can seem so distant and empty. Yet joy is still yours and it WILL come again.

Everything God created in the universe is in balance. Light is separated from darkness, sea from land, earth from sky. As day follows night, so joy follows sorrow.

Why pain? Why heartbreak? Why so much suffering in the world? For healing, for victory, for the opportunity to love. Empathy requires an understanding that can only come from the experience of pain.

Still at times I cannot fathom the need for such great grief as I have seen around me, but I know my faith is stronger because of it. Why am I told by the Holy Spirit to pray a specific prayer for someone in the middle of the night? Why does God place on my heart the need to intercede on their behalf when He could just as easily take care of the problem without me? He knows what the need is, why is He telling it to me? So I can be used by Him.

"God turned the captivity of Job, when he prayed for his friends." Job 42:10

God desires not only relationship with us but for us to have relationship with each other. To be the conduit to Him for others when they have no strength of their own, even the strength to pray.

When there are trials in my life, I often feel like I simply cannot bear the weight of them. Yet I don't have to bear them alone, I cry out for help and God sends it. People are praying for me and that comfort has brought a glimpse of the true joy I know will be mine again.

"For I consider that the sufferings of this present time are not worthy to be compared with the glory which will be revealed toward us. For the creation waits with eager expectation for the children of God to be revealed. In the same way, the

Spirit also helps our weaknesses, for we don't know how to pray as we ought. But the Spirit himself makes intercession for us with groaning's which cannot be uttered." Romans 8: 18-19, 26

Each wound of my life has actually made me into something altogether differrent, something stronger. A needle pierces my heart. Splits apart the fabric of my soul. Although the pain seems unbearable, the needle is preparing a space, making a place for the thread to go through, a thread that will connect me to another remnant, another experience of healing, and eventually of joy.

The following stories may seem disconnected and to some degree they are. They are simply snippets of a life not the whole. That picture is not yet finished and so cannot adequately be conveyed in any sort of cohesive manner. What follows are just some of the lessons I've learned and the beautiful things I've discovered along the way. A few tattered pieces, sewn together like a patchwork quilt. It is the thread running through all of them that has made my life into something extraordinary.

It is my complete and utter dependence on God, and an occasional willingness to allow Him to stitch me together again that makes my life, my existence more than just a remnant.

Remnant; *noun*
A small part or portion that remains after the main part no longer exists

HALFWAY TO HEAVEN

October 12, 2017

The "big" birthdays have never engaged my thoughts much. It's never the thirty or the forty that make me ponder, it's the ones just prior to them that make me take note, like the deep breath you inhale just before diving under the water. And so today, I am forty-nine.

I was born in Riverside California, the city where my mom and my grandmother were born, we all went to the same elementary school - at least for a moment.

You see my grandmother lived and died within a five-mile radius of her birth, which makes the life I've lived all the more unlikely.

Three of my grandparents lived well into their 90's and the other lived into her 80's. So, with that in mind it hit me today, on my forty-ninth birthday, that I may in fact only be halfway through this life.

The first feeling I experienced at this realization was sheer amazement. Then a little voice in my head said, "You have so much time, you can do so much more."

Time can make you feel old - perhaps older than one should feel, because it seems to go faster the longer you've been here. So, the first forty-nine years of my life felt like they took forever, yet looking ahead towards the next forty-nine finds me feeling like I'm racing against time itself.

I have lived a full life already and if I live only half as much in the second half as

I did in the first, well I will probably die of exhaustion.

I celebrated my first birthday on the Gila River Indian Reservation where my parents served as foster parents to several teenage boys in need of a family. Actually, my parents celebrated my birthday not me, because face it I was only twelve months old and pretty much oblivious, my brother and sister were still not thrilled at the idea of my existence, and the Indian boys living with us only wanted my parents to leave the room for a minute, so they could continue to torture me by holding me upside down and shaking me. Ah, the joy of one's very first memory.

A few years later and I had one birthday in Albuquerque, one back in Riverside, and not yet six the real adventure of my life began.

Four birthdays in Malaysia, four in The Philippines and by my fifteenth birthday I had lived in three states, three countries and twelve houses.

Rialto, Whittier, Fullerton, La Miranda, Hacienda Heights. By my "surprise" 18th birthday party sixteen houses. I've had several "surprise" parties thrown with great glee by my mom and sister. I used quotes around surprise because on the day of each party the giddiness with which they threw them gave them away.

I don't count the apartment I never stayed in, the one that was broken into and robbed the night before my wedding while my husband was at his bachelor party. Before I hit thirty I had added Tennessee to the states I have lived in and another seven houses as well.

I've slowed down quite a bit and have only added a few lately, so at forty-nine I've lived in twenty-eight places. The exhaustion is starting to make sense right?

I've been a bride, a wife and a widow.

I've given birth to three boys who have grown into young men who impress not only me but anyone who gets to spend just a few minutes with them. Every single day my heart breaks wide open with love and gratitude that I was chosen to raise these men.

I've hiked into a volcano, slept on the battlefields of WWII, played Duck-Duck Goose with Vietnamese children too young to be refugees and have been bitten by a monkey - twice!

I've started my own business and watched the music industry I loved almost disappear completely.

I've been to most of the states and more than a dozen countries.

I've been on tour buses with all kinds of musicians including being trapped one night in my RV on Rte. 66, during the remnant storms of hurricane Ike, with The Lost Dogs listening to my birthday buddy Michael Roe tell jokes that would make a 12-year-old boy proud.

I've been dead broke, well-to-do and

watched my husband's life insurance, what I was to live on for decades, shrink rapidly in a stock market crash. (A crash I missed the first three days of because I was in that RV with those Dogs.)

I've had surgeries and procedures, scary test results, hospital stays and have been told by more than one doctor that I will most likely live a long and healthy life, but I will be in pain for all of it.

So, I am forty-nine, a number that should scare me, right? But it in no way does, because I might just have another forty-nine to go, and I've still got so much to do.

Occasionally I get the feeling that I haven't done enough and that I may have been wasting the time I've already been given - until I start looking back at all the things I have actually done and seen.

As I sit here today, once again dead broke, unable to find full time employment and close to bankruptcy I realize my adventure may only be beginning. Standing on the precipice of what the world sees as failure, I am starting to see the freedom of it. There is still so much to learn and experience. I've never experienced the defeat of bankruptcy, but I'm sure there are emotions and lessons in it that I will make use of.

"What's the worst thing that can happen". That's the question my husband and I used to ask ourselves before we had kids, when we would look at our zeroed out bank account - bankruptcy we thought, but we can always rebuild. The worst thing that could happen, at least for my children already did. Failure, bankruptcy, losing a possession wasn't even on the scale of watching my children's father die in front of them. So now here we are, survivors.

If the Lord continues to bless my remaining family with good health, then the worst thing that can happen isn't happening to me - so it's time to get on with it.

At twelve I was prophesied over and have only seen parts of that prophecy fulfilled. Sometimes I wonder if any of it was really even meant for me, then I remember King David.

I have been thinking a lot lately about King David, anointed to be king at twelve, but years, decades go by and he is nowhere near his destiny, or so he may have felt.

What were the intervening years like for David? To go from anointed shepherd to the glory of being at court, to having the King, who was actively trying to murder him, walk into the cave he was hiding in.

What must David have felt along the journey? Maybe "Please Lord, go 'bless' somebody else with destiny already!"

It would be thirty-two years from the time David was anointed King, to his actually accession to the throne. But those years were never wasted, they were part of the plan. I'm guessing David at twelve would have made a king not much better than Saul. But a man pushing fifty, who had walked straight into the shadow of the valley of death? Now there's a man God can use.

I'm forty-nine, and I haven't even written my first book yet! Is that a waste of time, or simply patience in allowing the experience of my life to grow and mature as I search and reach for wisdom?

There is something remarkably freeing about standing right in the middle of one's life, half the journey behind you written in memories, half the journey ahead down a road mired in fog, unknown and undiscovered just waiting for your feet to make an impression.

The paths I've already walked filled with pain and comfort, love and hate, anger and forgiveness are not ones I would have expected or chosen if I had been given the choice at birth. I'm sure I would have picked an easy road, smooth and surrounded by roses and boring as can be.

Now pushing fifty, I might just be worth something. So, I'll take the fear of the unknown, the dust and the grit, the losses and the glory. I'll take the road God gives me, and with prayers and grace I'll make something amazing out of the years to come.

Anyone blessing me with birthday wishes today, well I only wish one thing - that we all go take the challenge of finding a way, big or small, to be the answer to someone's prayer for help

FALLING INTO FAITH

He that observes the wind, shall not sow, and he that considers the clouds, shall never reap. Ecclesiastes 11:4

Sometimes it is not a leap of faith that is required of us, but a falling into faith itself.

I recently watched the movie "City of Angels" again. I hadn't seen it in years but as I was flipping through channels, searching for something worthwhile to put on in the background while I did some chores in the middle of the afternoon there it was. It's a fine film with an incredible soundtrack, so I left it on and continued about my day, cleaning up toys, working on the computer, folding laundry not paying that much attention to it until it occurred to me what the entire point of the movie is. Not so coincidentally it's something that's been floating around in my head for over a month.

"City of Angels" is about an angel in Los Angeles who falls in love with a doctor trying to save a dying patient he has come to escort to "the other side". He spends almost the entire film wrestling with the decision of whether to become mortal, so he can be with her.

As an angel he is able to appear to her, talk to her, interact with her, but he has no earthly body with which to experience the wonders of earth. He cannot touch her. He wrestles with the choice. Give up everything he knows and is comfortable with to experience everything he has never had; or remain content with the known, the safe - certainty. There is a comfort in familiar, safety is there too. Will he choose what he is accustomed to or the adventure that is unknown?

It is a torturous process for him, but he finally decides to fall. That is what he has to do, literally fall into being human. It is not a leap of faith, it's a surrender into it.

Did you ever play the game of "Trust" when you were a kid? You close your eyes, keep your body perfectly stiff and straight, lean backwards and simply fall towards the floor. Your friends are supposed to catch you before you hit. I remember as a small child being just inches from the marble floor of our living room before someone caught me, I don't however remember having any sense of fear. I think it was the true faith of a child that I had at six years old, something life managed to gradually strip away from me little by little, year after year.

For our angel becoming mortal is not unlike that game of Trust, he stands on the edge of a building and chooses, in faith, to simply fall. He falls, ending up on the ground, bleeding, broken and overwhelmed with joy at the taste of his own blood in his mouth. He rushes to find her, struggling now through the obstacles of humanity that are completely new to him and when he finally meets her again they embrace and live happily ever after...

Except they don't.

They spend just one afternoon together, a blissful passionate day. Then suddenly on her way home from the store where she has gone to buy him a pear, because she wants him to experience every taste for himself - she is hit by a truck and killed.

He fell to become mortal, in order to love; and was given one afternoon of having it all, then just as abruptly he loses everything he fell for. It seems like a Shakespearean tragedy but the sense I come away with after watching this movie is that everything he has gained is still worth the fall. He has in front of him a lifetime of experiences yet to be his. Wonders lay before him that he could never imagine. Because you can never sufficiently describe to someone else the taste of a pear. Now he can taste it for himself, feel the warmth of the sun on his skin, know the gentle loving touch of another, and experience a life filled with uncertainty.

At the end of the movie he goes to the ocean at sundown. Angels gather here every night to listen to the sunset, they hear music in it, a sound humans will never hear, our fallen angel will never experience that joy again. But as the angels stand listening he walks past them into the water and begins floating on his back, his face serene, aglow in the amber sunset. The angels turn their gaze from the setting sun to look at him curious. They will always be able to hear the sunset but they will never experience the serenity he finds in it now.

There are no guarantees with faith, what we have fallen for may not be what we end up with. But true faith is surrender – complete and total. It is giving up all control and abandoning any expectations of what you may reap from the actions taken in that faith.

It's difficult while stuck in a mortal body to make choices and not first consider the earthly ramifications of decisions that are actually meant to be made with the eternal in mind. To live a life focused on eternity requires exactly that, an uncommon faith quite often leads to an uncommon life.

That is how we are to come to God, with the confidence a child would have trusting that He will be there when we fall, that He will catch us before we hit rock bottom, and that whatever life offers us is worth the risks of living it. Life is a gift, and we, in faith, are meant to simply fall into it.

ART

A few weeks ago, I turned on the stereo in my van and heard Bob Dylan coming through the speakers. I don't own any Dylan I'm ashamed to say, the CD belonged to my nephew Christopher. My sister had borrowed my van the day before and as usual her 15-year-old son, Chris had left behind a mix CD. Four Bob Dylan tunes abruptly followed by some screamo band; quite a rude awakening for me.

I smiled as I listened to Blowin' in the

Wind, Knockin' on Heaven's Door, and Ballad of the Thin Man. Not so much because they're incredible songs I hadn't heard in a long time, but because my nephew had "discovered" Bob Dylan on his own.

A week later we were driving together for several hours, he had been playing his screamo/hard core music just a little too long for me so I put on Peter Gabriel's "So", he suffered through it well enough. When it was his turn to pick a CD again I begged for something we could both agree on, he brought out the Dylan.

We listened and discussed the lyrics and how his voice had changed over the years. Christopher had read a book about him, I had recently seen the documentary by Martin Scorsese. This music isn't forty years old to Christopher, its brand new. Every lyric, every note could have been written yesterday.

Watching someone get excited about something you've taken for granted for years makes you appreciate it as if it were new to you as well. One of the most amazing things about music, any art form actually, is its ability to transcend time. My nephew and I don't agree on much music, but Dylan proved to be common ground between Underoath and Peter Gabriel.

Art, almost every kind, is extremely important to me and I seem to find it everywhere. I believe the manifestation of God's artistic expression is us. The ability to create art is one of the greatest gifts He's endowed human beings with. We are created in His image, and art is the outward expression of the human soul. Is it sacrilegious of me to say we are continuing what God started with our creation, when we use the abilities He gave us to create?

Even the Universe when looked at through mathematics is art. In an interview with Stephen Hawking he mentions Einstein's Special Theory of Relativity, smiling he said, "It's so beautiful it has to be right." Hawking sees God in the equations of physics, I hear God in music. I do not understand the creative process of writing a song, nor do I understand the physics of the universe. But I will always be awed and inspired by them both, because in them I see the beauty of God's creativity.

The creative expression that impacts me the most, will always be music. Sometimes I'm stunned by how profoundly music affects me. There are so many songs that have connected my heart and my thoughts to my memories. But there has also been music in my life that lifted me out of where I was, to somewhere beyond my experiences.

The music during the flying bicycle sequence in E.T. makes me believe in magic, but it's the final scene of farewell that always makes me cry. First with the sadness of goodbye, then with wonder and awe that I can still believe in the special friendship of an awkward grey alien and a wounded little boy. It's a wonderfully crafted movie, but it is the music that emotes those feelings. The end of the theme is remarkably emotional. The melody carried by a lone flute, taken over by French horns, echoed by a single trumpet, joined by tympani then the entire orchestra into crescendo. It doesn't matter how old I am; I will always believe in E.T.

Five notes into any John Williams theme from a Spielberg film and I'm overwhelmed again, with the same emotions I was full of walking out of the theatre. Blown away by the wonderment of Jurassic Park. Knowing the human spirit will always triumph after watching Empire of the Sun. Being unable to move, filled with too many emotions at the end of Schindler's List. Go back and listen to the anguished, lamenting cries of Itzhak Pearlman's violin, and you may be astounded at the emotions it will stir in you once again. Scientist say the sense of smell is the strongest sense we have that is linked to memory, but I think they've forgotten about John Williams.

Two years ago, I stopped at the post office on the way home. A new CD from The Choir was waiting. I didn't know what to expect, it seems every album they've put out in the last fifteen years has been a surprise. But even knowing that, I was taken aback.

The third song ripped at my heart. Even before Derri Daugherty's sweet and empathetic vocal began, some kind of sadness in the drums pulled me into it. I listened to it three times sitting in the driveway.

"She's Alright" was written about a woman going through a divorce. The beginning of the third chorus, Derri's voice is almost alone, it hit me hard and I found myself weeping.

I was going through a divorce, which may have been part of the reason those emotions were so easily brought to the surface. But hearing Derri sing those lyrics, knowing that he had also recently been through a divorce and knowing how much he still cares for her, I think I was crying for him as much as myself. I called him immediately and asked how in the world he was able to sing that song. He said nonchalantly it's what he does, he's a professional. I'm still amazed. I don't listen to it often; I can't get through it without weeping. Steve and Derri were once again able to craft a song, that made me feel sorrow, joy, hope and grief all at once. It's a rare and precious gift.

There is one song, which is probably more special to me than any other, because of my experience with it. You may laugh but it's "Return to Pooh Corner" by Kenny Loggins. I've always thought "Winnie The Pooh" had the greatest wisdom of all cartoon characters.

While pregnant with my first child I went through my hope chest and found my favorite teddy bear, I've had it since I was six years old. I took it out, being careful not to loosen the button eye that was about to fall off and placed it on a shelf above the crib. It triggered the memory of that song, so I found the album and the last three months of my pregnancy I played and sang that song to my son every day.

I had an easy pregnancy, but it was a difficult birth. Many complications left me weak and barely able to sit up for several days. The night we brought my son home from the hospital, he wouldn't stop crying. He'd been fed, changed and swaddled, but neither his father nor his grandmother could get him to settled down. I managed to sit up and said, "Give him to me." They placed him in my arms and I began to sing to him.

I looked into my son's eyes, he looked up at me, stopped crying and I saw in those eyes the recognition of who I was. He knew me because I was singing our song. It was at that moment that I became a mother.

For the rest of my life when I hear that song, it will trigger the memory of him cradled in my arms, a memory so strong I can almost feel him there still. No matter how old he gets, that's where he will be, at least in my heart.

So, if you are an artist and believe your art is not important, be bolder. If you feel you have nothing new to say, be braver. If you think no one cares about what is in your heart, be more honest. But please know that it is not just a song to me, those are moments of my life you are playing.

There are great songs out there waiting for me to discover them. There is also music that has not yet been written. Whose writer may be at this very moment, experiencing the joy or agony, that will someday when penned and put to a haunting melody, stir something in my soul, bring me to tears, and heal my broken heart.

I WONDER...

Have you ever just had "one of those days"? I'm having one of those days. One of those days where you swear the next glass of milk spilled on the bills will be followed by you leaving the kids at the neighbor's house and heading to a padded room somewhere?

The kind of day when I decide, no matter how it's been going thus far, I will salvage this waste of a day and make brownies with the kids. Yea that'll do it. We'll spend some quality time together and at the end, well, we'll have brownies!

So out comes the brownie mix. I let one child carefully cut the package open, another one slowly pours the mix into the bowl. Turn around to grab the measuring cup, turn back, and though not five seconds have passed, now everything and everyone in the kitchen is covered in a fine mist of chocolate powder. Here now I am faced with a typical parental dilemma. How do I react? Scolding, angry, laughter?

"How, HOW in the world did this happen" I inquire....calmly, rationally.

It's obvious who the guilty party is, he's smiling. He smiles when he lies, he smiles when he cheats, he smiles when he does anything wrong. I've accepted this and am planning my retirement around visiting days at the nearest minimum-security prison.

"Did you blow on it?" I ask.

"Yes" Devin says sheepishly, still grinning.

"Why" I ask.

Only giggles....

"WHY?" I ask again, now sternly.

"I wanted to see what would happen" he says with an innocent sweetness that washes from my mind all the terrible motives I have ascribed to his childish actions.

I absolutely love that my children say, "I wonder what would happen if...." when a new situation presents itself. The problem I have is me. Being an adult, I tend to think as an adult. Obviously, blow on it and we will all be covered in chocolate powder. I do realize however that I probably learned this as a child - by blowing into a bowl full of brownie mix.

Sometimes I just want my children to know things without my having to clean up the mess or the blood. Learning to stand back and watch them make messes, make mistakes, fall out of the tree I know is too difficult for them to climb, is a problem with me. I have years of experience, and I would love to simply, by stating the facts, impart it all into them so they wouldn't have to experience any of life's pain or messes for themselves. But things learned by experiencing them are somehow learned stronger. There's plenty of knowledge a child can attain from books and a parents warning but experiencing it for yourself makes a much stronger impression in your brain - that's how true learning happens.

Explain to a child how compressing CO_2 creates a very cold solid state that slowly returns through an endothermic reaction to a gaseous state and they may hear you. They may even remember what you said. But go buy some dry ice and make plastic water bottle "bombs", or put some water, liquid soap and dry ice into a bowl and make giant "cloud" filled bubbles to pop, let them watch as the solid dry ice slowly evaporates back into a gas, and they may actually understand the term endothermic reaction. Because they experienced it.

How amazing that God created us, is omnipotent but loves us enough to stand back and allow us to experience life. As a parent I have caught a small glimpse of the value of it and am reminded every single day that there is pain. My life is a mess, not because God doesn't love me enough, but *because* God loves me enough.

So, I'll continue to clean the messes, rush to the hospital for stitches, and learn to bite my tongue, stand back and watch when my children say, "I wonder what would happen if…".

Besides what's the worst thing that could happen, we might all end up covered in chocolate, and I for one can think of worse ways to end the day.

MAGIC ROCKS

When I was 14 my dad surprised us when he came home with a new invention, a video game that plugged into our TV - Pong. Remember Pong? It was revolutionary, and also rudimentary. It fascinated me more than entertained me, I was more interested in trying to figure out how this thing worked than actually playing it. Now Pacman, there was a game I could get into.

I remember playing some video game years ago with my nephew when he was still a little boy, and more interested in things controlled by microprocessors than things controlled by estrogen. He kept telling me to do absurd things that made no sense to me.

"Jump on that mushroom."

"What?" I'd say.

"Jump on that mushroom."

So, I did and I got money, some extra lives, or something, I don't remember what exactly.

Through the entire game he's barking instructions at me "Now pick up that rock."

"Ok what do I do with it?"

"Just keep it, you're going to need it later."

So there I am, jumping on mushrooms holding this rock. Why? Because my nephew had played this game before, through trial and error he had found all of its little hidden secrets and knew that rock was a magic rock and I could later use it to destroy the antagonist who was waiting just around the next corner.

I stopped playing video games. I didn't enjoy them and I hated having to play and die repeatedly just to figure out that in a different game I would have to pick up the mushroom and jump on the rock!

But I've realized lately, going about my life and watching my boys amuse themselves with new illogical distractions plugged into our TV, that video games are in fact a great allegory for life. Every stupid little action you are required to take in a video game does have a purpose in the end, the designer created it that way.

The trick is to keep playing until you've learned what bits and pieces of the game are actually the tools you're required to pick up and carry with you because in the future you're going to need them to get past an obstacle looming in front of you. You have to hold onto them until you can utilize them, even if that means clutching a rock while bouncing on a mushroom.

Similarly, our lives are fraught with peril but God has given us the tools we need to win long before we need them – we just have to figure out what they are, and when exactly to use them.

I walk through life and continue making the same mistakes. I keep having my essence disintegrate right in front of my eyes, because I've turned left instead of right.

Why does my life seem so familiar sometimes? Because I've already been here. I recognize and even anticipate the pain of my imminent demise, because I've already experienced it again and again. Yet, foolishly, I continue to think that the situation I've gotten myself into is completely new and the end of my world as I know it, I will surely never recover this time. How quickly we are to forget what we have already lived through and the lessons once learned.

The older I get the more Deja Vu I experience. I've been here so I remember it, I just didn't figure it all out in the first round, so I crashed and burned and had to start right back at the beginning, trying to learn this lesson again. This time will I finally notice the absurd out of place things randomly lying in my path? Probably not most of them. I'm too busy running straight into danger to slow down and pick up a rock, even a magic one.

As I get older I'm also beginning to get a little slower. My knees creak, I'm tired and sometimes I just need to sit down – which turns out to be true blessing from God. As I walk this road I've sprinted down a hundred times I can see things that I never noticed before. The road hasn't changed, I have. The tools I need in the next chapter are lying at my feet and now walking unhurried I've time enough not only to notice them, but to stop and wonder of what use they might be to me in the future.

I have played this game of life long enough to realize that I will be crushed by the antagonist again and again, probably just around the next corner. It's his only job and he's pretty good at it. If I stop to stare at a rock for a moment, or even sit and take the time to contemplate its purpose here in my path there is nothing lost, only wisdom is to be gained by a measured contemplative pace. The game continues on the same no matter how long it takes me to reach each chapter.

I've also realized that God has put a reset button in all of us and we get more than one chance. Every time I am crushed, if I play wisely, I learn a little something about the game, and this game unlike those video games I hate so much, is for keeps. This game is my life, and I plan on winning in the end. After all, I've got magic rocks, lots of them.

BEING JONAH

REALIZATION

[Arise, Go to Nineveh](#)
Jonah 1:2

"What was that like?" I asked.

"It was like being Jonah, it was an overwhelming experience."

A friend was telling me about hearing God. Now when most people say that they are speaking metaphorically. We usually refer to a "hearing" of God when we are having somewhat of a leading, not an actual physical experience. Mike had had a very in body experience, not ethereal, but physical. A very clear and powerful directive from God Himself telling him to move to Sacramento. Hearing Mike talk about it some thirty years later I could see it still freaked him out a little, it freaked me out too. Not because I didn't believe him, but precisely the opposite, I did believe him and that requires a completely different set of rules to govern your life by.

I have often thought that if God would simply tell me exactly what to do and where to go, I would quite happily walk along content in the knowledge that I was right where I was supposed to be, and perhaps somehow life would be easier.

Honestly though, after my conversation with Mike I wasn't so sure I wanted that anymore. Knowledge comes with a responsibility to take action. Knowing exactly what is expected of you can be frightening, especially when there seems to be no common sense to it.

Mike Roe is an incredible guitar player and songwriter who knew from the time he was a teenager that he wanted to use his music to bring people to God, now that same God was telling him to move to Sacramento. Sacramento in the 70's wasn't exactly a magnet for great musicians. No one in his right mind would move from San Francisco to Sacramento to jumpstart their musical career. So Mike, using logic, rational, and tinged with a bit of fear, did not move to Sacramento. At least not immediately. Instead he found himself not too much later in the belly of his own whale – a psychiatric hospital in Southern California. God will get us where He wants us to be, by any means necessary.

By the time Mike finally arrived in Sacramento, Warehouse Ministries had been growing for nearly five years. Patterned after Calvary Chapel Costa Mesa, "The Warehouse" as it was known, was not only home to legendary Saturday night concerts but soon their studio was pumping out some of the best music on the cutting edge, Christian or otherwise. One of the first albums they released was "Ping Pong Over The Abyss" by The 77's, a band fronted by Michael Roe.

I honestly don't know if Mike has fully realized yet how his listening to God has affected so many individuals, I personally know quite a few of them. One of my dearest friends, Van has told me on more than one occasion that the album "Ping Pong over the Abyss" helped him "get through" high school. He listened to it so much he wore out two copies.

Last summer I left him a voicemail at midnight while standing at the side of a stage at the Cornerstone Music Festival in Illinois. I couldn't wait to tell him that I was there watching the 77's play again. Van called me the next week and said when he listened to that message he almost cried. Like so many of us Mike ended up right where God wanted him, though not before first running away, just as Jonah had.

CONFIRMATION

<u>Proclaim the message that I give you</u>
Jonah 3:2

Which brings me back to Jonah, or rather God brought me back to Jonah a week later. I'll admit after talking to Mike I thought I should go back and read Jonah again. It's only four chapters after all, but I've seen the Veggie Tales version several times, I know the story, I grew up with it. What else could I possibly learn by reading it again? So I didn't.

I hadn't been to my little church for a few weeks, and so I was pleased to see the place overflowing once again on this Sunday night. After worship Tommy invited a young man to come up to give his testimony, something that happens on occasion in our church. He was in his early thirties, and his name was Jonah.

Jonah had one of those stories that I cannot relate to at all but am still awed by. The wounds of his life had left him at a point where he was addicted to drugs and doing everything he could do to get the money to buy them. He had been to church, had felt the need for a change in his life, but drug addiction is a beast and it wouldn't let him go. Jonah was so broken he felt that he wasn't worthy of salvation or love.

Fortunately, about ten months before he was caught with drugs and stolen property and was hauled off to jail. The arresting officer told him she saw something, sensed something in him that was different. He was a good person she thought, he just needed a chance to get past his drug problems.

She asked him if there was anything else she needed to know, anything else he needed to come clean on. "No" he told her bluntly. She told him to clean up his life and that she believed he could do it. The next morning waking up in jail, facing five felony charges, God worked a miracle in Jonah's heart. He knew now, beyond a cerebral knowledge, but a true knowing, that God loved and forgave him. "He put in my heart that He loved me," Jonah said. "That I didn't have to hurt myself anymore. And I was able to quit drugs, quit smoking, quit drinking." He was released on bail five days later.

What Jonah did next is what so amazed me. He went home, stood in his house and looked at an additional four thousand dollars-worth of stolen merchandise. He knew what he had to do, God was telling him what he had to do. "Take it to her" God said.

What would you do?

Jonah listened to that voice. "God put it in my heart that I had to take it to the police department and take it all to this woman that I had lied to, who was giving me a chance. I packed up four thousand dollars-worth of stolen electronic equipment in my mom's car. My mind was just screaming, 'Don't do this, sell this on the street, get rid of it.' (But) God was telling me 'You have to turn this in, face the music for what you have done,' only then could I move on and get healed."

So, Jonah walked back into the police station that night, found the Sergeant who had arrested him, believed in him, trusted him and this time came completely clean. Miraculously, when he left the station, he was facing only the original five felonies. He had done the right thing, finally, and that weight had been lifted.

"Jonah believed he had no character of his own, so God was going to make him do things His way to prove to him he does have character." Tommy Green.
October 8, 2006

A few weeks later, while driving to a one-day temp job at Home Depot, Jonah asked God to "Let me be a light, an example of what You want a Christian to be." Several hours later while stacking cinder blocks a woman approached him.

"You're a Christian aren't you?" she asked out of the blue.

"Yeah, I am," he answered - a little stunned at the proclamation.

"You're just like a light," she said "Your kindness and everything that you're doing; you're just like a light, I could tell you were a Christian."

Jonah started to cry, "It was like my Holy Father reached out and gave me a hug and encouragement in everything I was trying to do."

Because Jonah had courageously done the right thing, the sergeant who had sensed in him a depth of character, recommended leniency. Five felony counts were reduced to one, and instead of jail time he was given three years of probation.

Tommy returned to the microphone and said that because he'd been talking to Jonah earlier that week he had been inspired to go back and read the book of Jonah and was going to teach about it that night. Apparently God was going to tell me what I needed to hear, one way or another.

When Jonah (the one from the Bible) heard quite clearly the voice of God telling him to go to Nineveh and tell the people that they were to repent or be destroyed, there were many reasons he didn't want to go. The main reason however, seems to be that Jonah hated the Ninevites and did not want them to have the opportunity to be saved. He knew God was merciful and would hear their pleading. At the end of the book he is furiously screaming at God, asking why He had allowed them to repent.

But it displeased Jonah exceedingly, and he was angry. He prayed to the Lord, and said, "Please, Lord, wasn't this what I said when I was still in my own country? Therefore, I hurried to flee to Tarshish, for I knew that you are a gracious God, and merciful, slow to anger, and abundant in loving kindness, and you relent of doing harm. Therefore now, Lord, take, I beg you, my life from me; for it is better for me to die than to live." Jonah 4:1-3

I never saw myself as having any

similarities with Jonah, until Tommy began to talk that night. He spoke as he often does, of the big picture and our inability as human beings to see it. The fact is that God sees things in His eternal light, and we are temporal creatures and extremely shortsighted. Tommy went on to say:

"Nineveh centuries later became the capitol of Assyria, the same country that God ordained to come and judge the Israelites. It's interesting because Jonah didn't realize his place in history, God sends a dude in there years before we see them become who they are, and who they were was bad. So even in the roots of the nation of Assyria, at one-point God had sent someone in there to tell them who God was.

'This is the best part. Jonah doesn't realize that the things that God does in him over the next forty years could result in impacting lives generations later. Just like

'Jonah didn't realize that preaching to the

Ninevites and having them switch, he didn't see that as having anything to do with (Israel) later on. It's all a part of the plan.

'Jonah you have no idea who you're going to effect. But the reality is, because of the message that God puts in our hearts you share that with what God has given you and you let God deal it out. You don't know, but you could flip the whole destiny of families, and people, and scenes and cultures.

'If you don't understand that God has set us here for just a short period of time for a specific reason, you're going to feel like you don't have a place.

'You don't know what God has for you but every one of us has a destiny with God, He's ordained the days of your life. He knows where you're supposed to go and how you're supposed to get there."

ACTUALIZATION
Towards your holy temple
Jonah 2:4

I knew God was trying to tell me something. It was clear, as it usually is, that something was going on. But I'm human and therefore pretty darn stupid sometimes when it comes to spiritual matters. So, I waited quite impatiently and started looking for Ninevites.

I looked for them everywhere. That is everywhere I would have felt comfortable finding them. I would find myself screaming out loud, "Just tell me already" when God would put little reminders in my path to go to the Ninevites. Frankly I was beginning to get a little worried. Where was I supposed to go, what was I supposed to do?

It didn't take very long really, my Ninevite showed up a week later. Sadly, it was the last person on earth that I wanted it to be. It was the most obvious answer and it was right in front of me; it was too close, as close as my skin. Surely God wouldn't put this on my plate, I didn't feel like I had the strength for it, He must know that. It was my soon-to-be ex-husband. I sat still and prayed that there were Ninevites to be found elsewhere, and I desperately kept looking.

I have never been one that adheres to the idea that God creates pain in our lives. What I've learned, the experiences I've lived through over these past few years have revealed two things to me. What I want to believe and what I'm comfortable with are irrelevant to God. His character is constant, and He will do whatever it takes to put us on the right path, to place in front of us opportunity. Opportunity to become who He created us to be.

I had been separated for nearly three years and my marriage was over, completely. I considered myself to be divorced; the paperwork simply hadn't been signed. I had no hopes for any kind of reconciliation, my only hope was to somehow, someday land on soft ground. I longed for a relationship with Dave that would at the very least be civil both ways, for our sake and for the sake of our children. I never got it.

I knew how I should pray, I had known for years, but I was never able to bring myself to it. I knew I should pray that God would do whatever it would take to get my husband's attention. To soften his heart and break the hold that anger and resentment had on him. Anger and resentment towards me for leaving, towards his mother for dying, towards his father for giving up on life and pouring himself into a bottle.

I knew how I should pray but knowing something and doing it are two very different things. I knew in my heart from what I have learned of the character of God, that He would answer, and I knew the answer to that prayer would most likely wound my children. My instinct as a mother protecting her children took over, so I didn't pray. But my mother, someone stronger than me, had been praying.

One day at her Wednesday Bible study she shared with her group that she saw Dave as Saul, and she prayed that God would do what He had done to Saul on the road to Damascus - bring him to his knees.

The next day, December 14, 2006 while riding his motorcycle to work, a car pulled out in front of him. He hit it going thirty miles an hour, flew thirty feet through the air landing on the curb. He shattered his ankle, punctured a lung, broke several ribs, and collapsed both lungs; he nearly died. He was airlifted to USC Medical Center where the next day a CT scan was performed to check for additional internal injuries, what they found left everyone stunned, Stage IV lung cancer - terminal.

The moment I heard I knew what I had to do. I packed up my kids and when Dave was released from the hospital we moved back into the house I had left three years earlier in tears. I don't pretend to imply that it was easy, it was in actuality the most difficult thing I had ever done up to that point, even harder than leaving my marriage. But it wasn't a decision I made, I simply recognized where I had to go and I went.

God had led me to it. He had been preparing me for this moment for years. He had pushed me, shoved me, then cradled me in His arms. I had been allowed to fall, to fail, to suffer, and through it all God had taught me things in ways that gave me the strength to be a woman who could, with compassion, care for a man who had shown her none for years. But even as strong as I had become, this was still beyond me. It had to be done with complete and utter faith, it took more faith than I had to be able to walk back into that house, it took an army of prayers to hold me up.

For two months I had been listening to

Mike, Jonah and Tommy over and over again in my head. God was speaking to me through them. There was no audible voice as Mike had heard, but a quiet gentle knowing. On one hand going back was a very easy thing to do, because God was allowing me to see a glimpse of that big picture Tommy was talking about.

The future generation I would be influencing, that I would be effecting for decades by my action or inaction was my own children. I could look directly into the faces of the boys I had given birth to, whose characters were being formed through this experience, who would soon become men, men of God I hoped. I knew that what God had laid before me, was the opportunity to minister to them, by ministering to their father. I was given the gift to do something that would affect their future, the rest of their lives.

It is remarkable to me how God gives us through grace exactly the tools we need before we ever know we need them.

Because of His understanding of who I am, how He created me, He had whispered in my ear for weeks - "something's coming". He placed little things in my path knowing that I would string them together, that I would look for a clear picture from seemingly insignificant, unrelated events. My personality is to find commonality in random moments of my life, then try and chase them down to a singularity, at which point I start looking for the purpose in it.

That is the only reason that I had the strength for this. He had prepared the path for me, placed in front of me the tools I would need, led me to them, then let the decision be mine. I simply continued to do, what I have been striving to do for 32 years; hold onto to the hand of God and walk, reluctantly perhaps, where He was telling me to go. It was very much like being Jonah.

Dave died six weeks after being diagnosed. He had the opportunity to say goodbye to his children, to see how many people truly loved and admired him. He was given the gift of knowing that his time here was nearly over. He was able to make sure he made everything right, as right as you can make a life from your deathbed.

I don't pretend to know why Dave got cancer and died at forty-eight, leaving behind three young boys for me to raise alone, but I know God will use it for glory if we allow Him to. Dave and I were able to lay down most of the baggage we had picked up over sixteen years. We were able to show our children that no matter what, they were of the ultimate importance to us both and that God is holding them through it all.

I know that in the big picture, the one that I still cannot see clearly, God will use the wounds of my children's lives. The wounds I was so desperate to protect them from will become scars, that may someday help heal the hearts of others.

I don't think trapped in our humanity we can truly ever catch even a small glimpse of what is really happening to us. God our father does for us what may seem to be cruel sometimes, He allows us to experience the painful repercussions of a life lived by self-determination. But He also gives us direction along the way. Situations that may appear as roadblocks, which we may interpret as punishment or cruelty I think may be placed there to stop us, to cause us to make a turn sharper than we ever would have without a brick wall suddenly rising up in front of us.

God will use every loss, every hurt, all of our suffering to expose our purpose here. To rip away the veil of fear, the insecurity we cling to. He will draw us out, violently if necessary, to force us to use the gifts He has given us for eternal glory. To see ourselves as He does - worthy. We so often disregard as insignificant our abilities until we are cornered and required to use them as He walks us through the fire.

I have never been able to reconcile the reality of what my marriage was, with the reality that God had, years ago quite clearly told my husband and I both that we would marry each other. He spoke to each of us years apart and in different ways, and we both listened; yet what we made of that marriage seemed to be nothing that was of any use to God. But I know there is purpose in it.

I have always scoffed when people say they have no regrets because every decision they made has brought them to where they are now. But with age and experience I can now understand the sentiment of it. There are things I have done, decisions I have made, that I hope if placed in front of me again would see me making wiser choices. But even through my mistakes, my selfishness, my humanness, God has delivered me right where He wants me to be, here.

Perhaps there was a smoother road I missed which could have gotten me here as well, but I doubt it. I don't think I would be as useful to God, that I would be strong enough without having gone through that fire. As Tommy is fond of saying, "It's the wounds that make us who we are." I think he's right, but I also think it is how we experience the healing of those wounds that reveals the true depth of our character.

"I want people in my life who fall, because I need to see what it's like to fall down and get back up again."
Tommy Green

MILES AND MILES

All that is meant for destruction when laid at the feet of God with prayer and faith is returned to us as blessings. (Romans 8)

I have been through every human emotion there is in the past few months and just in the past three weeks the differing shades of grief I've experienced or been witness to have astounded me. There have been so many things to grieve and they all seemed so clear so vibrant as I sifted through a lifetime worth of photographs, trying to narrow them down, searching for a handful that would sum up a life.

What I found were memories of hopes, of dreams, of sorrows. The loss of innocence of my children. The loss of a marriage that seem to be derailed from the start. The faces of two hopeful people I could barely remember, but I did remember them. The starting out, still seeing mostly the good in each other. The wedding photographs, smiling, dancing, laughing; sharing a joke long forgotten, but the dreams of a bright future still clear on those faces.

The father holding his firstborn son as they stared into each other's eyes for an hour. A train ride to San Diego. Feeding the dolphins at Sea World. Three boys who couldn't wait to show their parents every seashell they found on the beach "Look mommy, this one looks just like the rings of Jupiter." The first flight on a jet plane, then the first plane ride with daddy as the pilot.

So many firsts to remember and yet so many still left to be experienced without him. A nine-year old boy, too grown up for his age now, "I keep thinking about all the things daddy won't be here for." The heart can break in so many ways it seems, even when it's already shattered.

A Grandmothers prayer, that her grandson would have dreams of his father in heaven, at peace. Then the answer found in the stars. The night of his father's memorial service, Miles came to me with a picture of him and his dad that he had drawn. He does this every night now, it is the only way he knows how to express himself, to ask his mom to hold him so we can cry together. To take the time to ask the questions that there are no good answers for, "Does daddy miss me as much as I miss him?" "I'm afraid that daddy is sad." 'Where is heaven?"

But this picture was different, every picture thus far was him standing next to his father. After two weeks the portrait of himself was the same...tears. But the expression he drew of his father had changed. No longer standing beside him, but above him now, kneeling on a cloud looking down on him and smiling. He had seen him in the stars he said, a small cluster that he knew was his father's smiling face, telling him he was ok. Then tonight a picture of the entire solar system with him standing here on earth and his dad, beyond the asteroid belt, Saturn and Neptune, in a small circle he labeled as heaven.

He is letting go. He is allowing the realization of the distance, the time, the sorrow to slowly seep into his heart. It is a painful road to walk with him, but we are not walking it alone. The prayers of the saints are poured out at the feet of God in Revelation, nothing is ever wasted with God. In the end those prayers are all returned to Him as songs of praise. (Rev 5:8)

I see that Shakespeare was right "All the world's a stage, and all the men and women merely players: They have their exits and their entrances; And one man in his time plays many parts." I've spent the last few weeks looking at the scenes that have played out in my life thus far. The curtain has come down on the second act of my life, but only the first act of the children's. What scenery will be on that stage as the curtain rises in the next few weeks is up to us.

"You have your whole life ahead of you," a friend told me Saturday. I do. I am only thirty-eight after all, yet I am a widow and a mother of three, my life is still being written and there is much still to tell.

The curtain is about to rise on the third act of my play. If I am blessed with a long life I know that I will someday sit in a rocking chair, reminiscing with my great-grandchildren at my feet. I will tell them of "the old days", when men did not yet live on the moon and I went through trials of fire that made me stronger, wiser, gentler; and that all these years later when I look back, I can see in every one of those moments, the merciful hand of God pulling me through.

A BEAUTIFUL MIND

My son Cole has a beautiful mind. It works in fascinating ways that often leave me in awe, but just as often leave me shaking my head unable to understand exactly how to reason and deal with him. Numerous teachers and speech therapist have told me that they have never encountered a child who has done things the way he does them.

On his first visit to his speech therapist she was amazed at the patterns Cole made of the stickers she gave him to decorate his folder. At first, he did not seem to be making anything in particular, but as she continued to hand him the stickers one by one, each of us could see he had had a plan from the beginning, though his beginning did not start where we would have expected it to. It was complete in his mind and it didn't seem to matter to him where he started or ended the creation, he always knew what it would be.

When he started pre-school last year he was almost five. When I went to pick him up at the end of his first day his teacher showed me his work. She had handed him a blank sheet of paper and asked him to draw his face. He drew eyes, a nose, and a mouth. He did not however place a circle around them; he had only drawn the features of his face not the outline. She was stunned, she had never in fifteen years of teaching encountered a child who had done that. "It's as if he has no boundaries," she said. I was thrilled. I saw it as typical Cole. She asked him to draw his face, not his head, if she had said to draw his head I'm sure he would have encompassed his facial features with an oval. In his mind he had done exactly what she had asked him to do. He is quite a literal individual.

Five months later at the year-end parent teacher conference she showed me the same picture and a recent one he had done. She was happy that now, when asked to draw his face he would first make a circle, then draw all his features inside of it. "See", she said quite pleased, "he's learned how to do it right." I almost cried, it actually broke my heart a little. They had managed to conform him to the "in the box" or rather the "in the circle" way of thinking.

I on the other hand have always loved the way Coles mind works; that it doesn't look like everyone else's is a beautiful thing to me, even when it frustrates me. He has always made me smile and look at things from a different perspective. Because of him I've seen things in a way I never would have if I didn't take the time, to get down on my knees behind him, follow with my eyes down the line of his outstretched arm to his pointing finger, and try to envision the way those things are appearing to him, translated in his very unique and different brain. I would never want to change that about him.

I'll admit that sometimes my son frustrates me so much it is hard to keep my eyes focused on his gifts. Cole was sick last week with a cold and I had to give him a decongestant before we could travel down the mountain we live on. I usually don't force medication on him because it is more than a struggle, but this day it was necessary.

He first bites my finger until it bled. Then when I asked my mom to help me hold him down so I could force the medication into his mouth he projectile vomited all over both of us and the bed as well. I went upstairs to change my clothes and when I came down five minutes later, he was standing in the kitchen staring at the bottle of medication. I asked him if he wanted to take it now. "Yes" he said flatly. He took it without so much as a hiccup.

Today the doctor told me he has a slight case of bronchitis and pneumonia. We caught it just in time, but he will need to take two different medications for ten days, seven doses a day, that's seventy doses of medication! Tonight, I spent over two hours dealing with the first two doses; I don't know how I'm going to get through the week.

I love him beyond words, but he is the most contrary child imaginable. He will argue with you that the moon is the sun until you give up, then he will simply look at you and say "Look, there's the moon."

Arrogance to believe in the impossible is how we got to the moon after all. The declaration was made that we would land a man on the moon in less than ten years when in actuality we had not one of the tools to do it. And yet it was done, because of tenacity, arrogance and thinking not outside of the box but as if there was no box at all. This is the mindset my son has, and I pray he is somehow able to keep it and still succeed in life. We will both have to fight constantly to not only allow him to be creative and think as an individual, but to somehow marry that to the way the rest of the world operates.

A few months ago Cole and I were driving down the road and he asked where we were going, I said we needed to go buy a new battery for the car. "The car doesn't have a battery" he informed me, "the car uses gas". I tried to explain, repeatedly, that the car uses gas to go, but a battery is needed to start it. He argued, and argued, and argued. I finally pulled the car over to the side of the road, took him out of his car seat, popped the hood and showed him the battery. "Oh." he said. That was it. We got back in the car and continued on our way.

My job as his mother is not to change the way his mind works but to teach him how to live in a world that will not always appreciate his beautiful way of thinking. To help him deal with those things that make him different and steer him down a path where his unique abilities will be held as treasures. To keep his tenacity, but to foster in him the ability to work with others while somehow maintaining the arrogance that he is right...until of course he is proven wrong.

"I have not failed 700 times. I have not failed once. I have succeeded in proving that those 700 ways will not work. When I have eliminated the ways that will not work, I will find the way that will work."
—Thomas Edison on building the light bulb

He will make a good lawyer, scientist, or inventor I think. Or perhaps he will become a teacher, and maybe one day a child will come into his class and do something in a way that no one ever has before. I think Cole would be one to appreciate that.

DAWN'S L.A. DAY

Last weekend my sister brought her kids up to my house in the hope of finding some snow. I live in the mountains surrounding Los Angeles, so snow is not an impossibility in January, only a misguided hope.

She works in Hollywood and spends most of her day in a small office with no windows, except the ones on her computer. Surrounded by people more concerned with their dogs than the people around them. Working tirelessly on music for soap operas, trying to convince herself she's not wasting her life. At lunch yesterday, on her way to the commissary she went downstairs opened the door to an unseasonably cool 63 degree LA day, and found - snow.

It seems that a scene set in a place that only exists on a television set called for snow, so they ordered snow. You see in Hollywood you can order pretty much anything you want, no need to hope or to have faith. Surrounded by actors, teamsters, fake sets and fake snow, she's off to lunch.

Six hours later, at home, she receives a phone call from a friend in Nashville. He's a songwriter in Christian music, and quite a successful one at that. He's been out drinking too much and is on a street corner looking at his car. A wise idea not to drive but what to do? He calls a friend, just to talk and say, "what an idiot I am". It's been a tough day for him as well. He spent the day writing songs with some up and comer he'd never met before, put together by a publishing company, in the hopes that they would click and write the next great worship song that will make them all a million dollars. A strange idea, almost as strange to me as snow in LA.

The parallels are not hard for me to see, but it's a sad realization that Hollywood and Christian music are so much the same. Both are based on what we want to see, not any sort of reality. The dichotomy between who God calls us to be and who we pretend to be is frightening.

There is nothing more real than our failure to be. To be real, to be honest, and to be unafraid of being judged by everyone around us. That's why, after all, everything is so fake in this world. We're comfortable with that, life's easier to swallow, coated as it were, with the sickening sweetness of lies.

There was no snow in LA last weekend, but don't worry, they were able to buy some. Me, I think I'll wait, until the sky sees fit to open up and pour out its own snowflakes, each one a tiny miracle, as beautiful and individual as all of Gods creations are.

BLUE JAYS, BULLIES AND THE BRAVE

Every spring a pair of blue jays come to our porch to make a nest behind one of the light fixtures. We watch them out the kitchen window, first bringing twigs to repair the damage the strong winter wind has done to the nest left from last year. Then splitting their time between looking for food and sitting on the eggs.

They will usually hatch three chicks occasionally four. At first we don't know the chicks have even hatched, it's a few days before we finally see their ugly bald heads atop skinny outstretched necks sticking up over the edge of the nest, beaks wide open, impatiently waiting for their next meal to be delivered. It only takes a few weeks for the feathers to come in, and then these tiny creatures to grow to the point that they begin to get uncomfortable in their nest. Three chicks fit nicely, three birds do not.

There is not too much notice paid to them until a couple start squawking so loudly you can't help but notice. Inevitably, every year there are two birds who refuse to leave the nest, full grown yet still waiting for their next meal to be brought to them. We never notice the one who flies away first, it has quietly just spread its wings and left, apparently hungry, determined and brave enough to venture out and find food on its own.

The pair that remains squawk incessantly for their mother to come back. She sits on a branch not too far off, squawking back to them, trying to lure them out. It is the same scene we have watched play out summer after summer. Two birds, much too big to be considered chicks, sit perched on the edge of their nest. No longer afraid of being seen, a look of confusion on their little bird faces.

Everything has changed. This is not the routine they know, and yet they will sit there for hours upon hours looking for the comfort of the normalcy. They have not yet realized or perhaps have simply not yet accepted what I know to be true through years of watching this same story over and over again through the kitchen window. She is not coming back. She is waiting, watching, calling, but she will not return. She knows they can fly they just don't know it yet.

I have watched my children fall flat on their faces - literally and figuratively. I can tell you watching them get hurt physically is much easier than watching them stumble out into a world filled with cruelty without me as their buffer. I want to walk beside them forever, through every part of their lives, but that is not my job.

Three months ago we took a family trip

to the eye doctor. I have always kept a close watch on my children's vision because I received my first pair of glasses at eight as did their father and virtually every aunt and uncle on both sides. So, when our insurance was about to change I decided that I could procrastinate no longer.

I expected to walk out of the office having been told that the older two needed glasses right now, with the question of why hadn't I brought them in sooner, as well as being told that the youngest was surely to follow suit soon. But I was mistaken, only one child needed glasses, at the familial appropriate age of eight, so I guess I wasn't too far off in my assessment of his genes.

What surprised me was that the other two, who did not need glasses both wanted them. They had come into the store expecting to get glasses and had already spent considerable time in the waiting room picking out several pairs for themselves. "Well it's a different world then the one I grew up in" I thought as we headed home, Devin beaming proudly asking when he would receive his new glasses. And yet, as it turns out, the world is not really so different from when I was eight-years-old.

I cringed the first day I sent Devin to school, his new spectacles perched atop his nose. I had the strongest memory of walking into my third grade class, which consisted of myself and four boys, and having the boy I thought was 'the cute one" announce to everyone in the first through third grades that I looked ugly. Would Devin now face that trial I wondered.

Off he went to school as I went home and held my breath. Seven hours later he came home, bounding down the bus steps, happy as a clam, everyone in his class had told him how great he looked. I thought his glasses suited him, and I breathed a sigh of relief that my son's friends thought so too. But all was not well.

Three days later, Devin slinked off the bus, shoulders heavy, no glasses on his face. At first, I was afraid he had lost them or broken them so as soon as he got in the car I asked where they were. "In the case in my pocket" he said. He proceeded to burst into tears. There was, as there always seems to be, a mean sniveling little boy on that bus, who was more than happy to be the first person to tell Devin he looked like a geek.

I tried to console him, but I wasn't much help. I tried to convince him that in the end life is sweet and the smart and kind ones will always win - somehow. I told him I had never dated any boy who didn't wear glasses, as much as he loves me, that didn't seem to matter.

Then I told him that the boy who had teased him was probably not nearly as talented or intelligent as him or he surely could have come up with something better than 'geek' to use as an insult.

Geek is a good thing these days after all, Bill Gates is considered a geek. Best Buy even named their repair service guru's the Geek Squad. The world finally loves geeks, we have to, we depend on them to fix the technology we've come to rely on to get through the day. The future now depends on the geeks of the world being successful and multiplying in order for the rest of us to survive. When my computer crashes, I want a code-speaking nervous Trekkie at my door, not the high school quarterback who didn't have enough imagination to date anyone outside of the cheerleading squad. I want someone who spent every Saturday night during high school learning to speak Klingon!

Devin got through it. Until he was ready to face the boy he would simply put his glasses in their case and put them on when he was off the bus and in the safety of his classroom. Eventually he didn't think about it anymore. The boy gave up, it's not much fun to tease someone who doesn't fight back. Devin had won by sucking it up and at the tender age of eight, became the better man.

Yesterday he got off the bus beaming again. On the drive home he said, "Do you remember that boy on the bus who teased me about my glasses?" "Yes" I said, "Is he bothering you again?" "No" Devin said, the eyes behind those glasses now shimmering with joy, "HE got glasses." We both laughed out loud – for a long time!

My job as a mother becomes tougher every day. I'm not there to fight every battle, sometimes I have to sit on a branch hiding behind some leaves. I can watch them, but I must let them be. I can call back to them when they cry out, let them know that I am close but that I am not going to pick them up and carry them this time. They are ready to try this one on their own, to see if there is air to be found under their untested wings. I know they can fly, but I have to let them figure that out for themselves. It's the fearful ones, who always end up making a racket, obscuring the brave. The fearless are already flying, quietly soaring along on the wind.

FILLING IN THE GAP

There comes a time in every person's life when a little assistance is required. When they encounter a gap in the road, no way around, with no feasible way across the chasm they are confronted with. Poised on a precipice which separates who they are from who they could be, if simply given the chance to reach the other side.

The distance may appear to them impossible to traverse, but the canyon they face may in actuality be quite small and crossed fairly easily with just a bit of help from another. Someone willing to fill in the gap.

The house in Grand Terrace was small, but bigger than the condominium they had recently moved from. Five bedrooms surrounding a small kitchen and living room, a pool and a garage that served as a rehearsal space for several local bands.

My sister Dawn made the 90-minute drive to LA every weekday, returning about 7:30 every night to what had become a haven for a few dozen teenagers from the surrounding towns, more than a dozen of whom now lived there. It began innocently enough a few years earlier on a routine trip to Walmart a few days before Christmas.

Dawn and her kids noticed a woman in a wheelchair being wheeled towards the space heaters. It was Lori and her son Tyler. Years earlier when Lori was Dawn's neighbor, she had on occasion needed help with her kids, Dawn had offered to help out, even keeping them for a few days when Lori was admitted to the hospital.

They hadn't seen each other in quite a while so Dawn and her kids stopped to say hello and catch up. Things had gone from bad to worse for Lori, who was soon going to be admitted to the hospital and had no place for her kids to go. At that moment they were living in a motel with no blankets and were hoping they could find an inexpensive space heater they could afford.

If there is one word my sister knows, it's yes.

That night Dawn began emailing friends asking for help in buying the family blankets, food and Christmas presents. A few days after Christmas Lori's two kids moved into the condo Dawn rented with her two kids. Soon there would be another boy needing a place to stay for a few days. Next a girl whose dad had kicked her out and had nowhere else to go. They would come to her when they needed a bed to sleep in, a shoulder to cry on, or a prayer said on their behalf.

There were several variations of "Dawns house" as we now refer to it.

The house on the main street of town, that the landlord wouldn't fix anything on because it was going to be torn down to make way for a fast food restaurant as soon as the permits came through. Then a three-bedroom condo, too small for all the kids who wanted to live there, then the "pool house", another teardown which ended up housing seventeen people at one point.

My sister has only two biological children, but for years she has "adopted" dozens of others simply by opening up her heart and her home to them. As a result, my parents are also considered grandparents by dozens of hard-core, tattooed and pierced kids.

My mom always delighted in cooking them special vegan and vegetarian dishes, not an easy task when you grew up on southern cooking. But she's quite creative and the kids are always surprised and appreciative when she makes them something they can enjoy with the rest of us.

Years ago, Dawn and I were in Nashville visiting some friends and not all of the kids in her small town knew that we were not in California that weekend. About 4:00 AM Dawn's cell phone rang. It wasn't one of her two kids or even one of the other dozen who were living with her at the time; it was Adam, Josh and Joseph, friends of her daughter. It had been snowing in the local mountains all day and always up for an adventure they decided to take a drive to check it out. They brought with them no chains, no snow tires, just excitement and the ignorance of youth.

It continued to snow all day and late that night as the boys tried to make it up and over the last hill before freedom was theirs, the reality of the situation smacked them square in the face. They ended up sliding into a snow bank and armed with nothing but their wits, could not get themselves out of it.

These boys are from San Bernardino,

where it rarely gets below 50-degrees so they weren't exactly dressed for 25-degree weather and ten inches of snow. Being in the mountains they also found themselves without cell phone service. So there they sit at two o'clock in the morning dressed, well – like teenagers from Southern California.

Luckily the people who live on this particular stretch of road are used to stranded motorists and actually sit on their porches when it snows to watch the "flatlanders" slide down the hill into each other. My mother and I were rescued in the exact same spot, by several teenagers who lived on this street not one week earlier. Not only did they bring shovels to dig us out, but their mom took me and my kids inside her home and gave them hot chocolate while her heroic children dug our truck out of the snowbank.

So, when these boys walked up to a house at two am, knocked on the door and asked to use the phone, they were welcomed in with open arms.

At four am in Nashville Dawn gets the call, "HELP!" She explained to Josh that she was two thousand miles away but that she would call her dad who lived nearby in the mountains to see if he could help. So, at 2 am my then sixty-six-year-old father, drags himself out of bed, puts the chains on his truck, loads up some coats, more chains and ropes and he's off to rescue some teenagers he's never even met.

He couldn't pull their car out that night so instead he loaded them into his truck and brought them home for the night. The next day he took them back to their car and called a tow truck, which managed to pull their car out of the snowbank. You would think when talking to these boys now about their little adventure that night, that they had been lost at sea for a week with no food or water and that my father had come steaming to the rescue bringing the entire US Navy with him.

A few months later as I casually related this story to an LA industry friend over dinner his first question was to inquire which of Dawn's kids it was.

"It wasn't one of her kids" I said "it was friends of her kids".

"Why were they calling her then?" he asked indignantly. I just sat there and stared at him confused.

"Because they knew she would help." I said. He couldn't believe it.

"They're not her kids she shouldn't be helping them; they should be calling their own parents."

I couldn't understand what I was hearing. I argued, to no avail, that they were after all somebody's children and human beings, ones deserving of help no matter how foolish their actions may appear. He was unwavering. They should not be rescued. In his opinion they should have been taught a lesson. I tend to disagree that being left in a car overnight in below freezing weather is an appropriate response to a teenager's reckless need for adventure; after all, it's exactly the type of thing my father would have done at sixteen

– or sixty-six for that matter.

It sure didn't seem like anything very significant to Dawn or to my dad, they have rescued people out of direr circumstances I assure you and on occasion have been in need of some rescuing themselves. They are always there when someone needs help, even at two am when it's snowing – it's just their nature to help someone when asked.

Upon hearing my friend's reaction, I began to wonder why it is such a difficult concept for so many in this day and age to understand, the simple idea of being a helping hand.

I do not understand the argument that a teenager in crisis is not my problem. If I don't take action when no one else does that teenager may fall through a gap and become everyone's problem. Prisons today are filled with many potentially good people who were left to fend for themselves when no one showed up to help bridge the distance. Stranded on the wrong side, I have often wondered who they may have become if they had managed somehow to reach the other side.

I have heard many people question the worth of not only my parent's life spent dedicated to other people's children, but now Dawn's tireless efforts on behalf of these kids. She worked a full time job, which was over an hour's drive from her home, yet she saw her real work, her purpose in life when she walked through her front door.

She tried on occasion to bring others in to help, but they usually want signed releases from parents saying it was okay to feed their kids, or take them to church or to a concert. One person even insisted he could not help unless they purchased liability insurance. Perhaps a prudent course of actions considering the wild and crazy Tuesday nights they all spent at Bible Study in Dawn's living room. These kids didn't come with disclaimers, they come with broken hearts.

Most people just stood in awe of her, as I always did. Many gave not only praise and prayers for Dawn's home, but furnishing, food and occasionally a little financial help as well. Some gave nothing, and that's okay too. It's the few who gave only criticism, who seemed overly concerned with the details, who have no understanding of why she did it, without grants or subsidies, it's those few who question the value in it at all that has confounded me.

Numerous people have asked me why she did it. They were there, they just showed up needing her.

Did she get money from the government or some organization to take in the kids who lived with her? No, most of them were over eighteen and just needed a place to stay for awhile.

What about the parents of these kids?

That is a question I do not have a complete answer for. Some came from wonderful homes; some have survived home-lives I cannot begin to relate to. But in Dawn's home they found complete acceptance of their music, their tattoos, the searching for their own identities.

My sister had on her wall the lyrics to a song entitled "Mercy Lives Here" by The Choir. She practices it and simply put that is the answer to why these kids kept showing up on her doorstep.

Dawn's cupboards were always bare. Several rooms in her house smelled like "teen-age boy". She got very little sleep, but she has never turned her back on someone in need. My parents and I helped out as much as we could; however we could. Most of the time it was just prayers, hugs and a shoulder to cry on, but occasionally it was a snowy midnight rescue at five thousand feet.

From time to time Dawn would find herself rescuing a child on the edge of that precipice, most often not even aware of the chasm they were about to fall into. We are now able to look back, years later, and see a clear picture of the broken road some were on. How the act of kindness may have kept them from falling in. It is in those moments that I truly understand how a simple gesture, an outstretched hand, can not only mend a heart but fill the gap as well.

All of this comes with a price.

After years of working to pay all the bills, then actually quitting her job to work from home so she could be there for the kids more, Dawns house ended. She was exhausted, broke, and unemployed. Dawn had quit a very good job with outstanding potential for growth and advancement in great part so she could continue to increase her work with these kids.

After the house closed, it took her several years, nearly a decade in fact, to just get a full time job, which ended up being back in the same department she had left. She was now at the bottom, in both pay and seniority. She paid a great price for her decision, the cost of which she will pay for the rest of her life. The cost was not paid by her alone. The cost was also shared with her children, who have paid heavily as well.

Paying a personal cost because of your parent's ministry is something Dawn and I are very familiar with. But my brother paid so much more than we did. In fact, he nearly paid with his life.

THE LIFE OF A HATCHET

The hatchet arrived in a brown box, along with some candy and birthday presents after an eight-thousand-mile journey from the United States to our new home in Penang, Malaysia. It was a small hatchet, but a strong one, solid metal from handle to head. It was purchased by our uncle Danny for our dad as a utilitarian tool to cut firewood on his camping trips with the Royal Rangers group he led, an organization something akin to the Boy Scouts.

It spent most of its life, as most hatchets do, uneventfully tucked away in a drawer full of tools just outside my parent's bedroom. But occasionally this particular hatchet would find its way out of that drawer and live an adventure.

About a year after the hatchet arrived uncle Danny and his wife Kathy came to visit us for the summer. In all the years we lived in Southeast Asia this was the first and last time we would receive a visit from family. It was simply too expensive a trip.

About a week into their stay we were all packing up one evening, preparing to drive to the mainland the next day and spend some time in the mountains.

We considered ourselves lucky in those days, we lived in paradise and though it was the third world, we still had hot water to take showers. Ours did not come from a central water heater tucked away in a closet or the basement though, each bathroom in the house had a small propane heater mounted on the wall next to the shower.

Earlier in the day, someone had cleaned the small window used to vent the excess Carbon Monoxide released by the water heater and inadvertently left it closed

My brother, Jim, had been taking a shower in our sister's bathroom, a very long shower, which was not at all unusual for him, but Dawn was getting tired of waiting. She knocked on the door, she banged on the door, she yelled for him to get out, all to no avail. Finally, she went out to the sunporch, climbed onto her dresser and peered into the bathroom through the tiny window near the ceiling.

She saw Jim, wet and naked, laying on the floor unconscious.

Dawn ran to my parent's room in a panic and told dad what she had seen. He dropped the bottle of Chloraseptic spray he was packing and even before it hit the floor, he was running to her room.

He forced the window open, went back

to the bathroom door and began throwing furniture at it. Nightstands, chairs, my sister's piano stool, all of them shattered like kindling against the solid wood door, nearly two inches thick. The door stood firm - not even a dent.

Danny and Kathy, sitting out on the adjacent balcony watching a rainstorm, heard screaming and loud crashes coming from the next room. Danny came running, with Kathy trailing behind him desperately trying to get my dad or Dawn to tell them what was going on. All he saw was my dad throwing furniture at the door in a panic. My dad, seeing his son on the floor, had in no uncertain terms lost it; it was Danny who said, "Do you have an axe?"

Not long after Danny and Kathy arrived, my mom and I got there from downstairs, we had heard the same God-awful noises and had run upstairs to find out what was going on.

We arrived to find my dad chopping a hole in the door. He made a large enough opening to reach through, unlock and open it. He picked up my brother's lifeless body, laid him on the bed and said, "He's not breathing."

I can remember that moment as if it happened yesterday. There is a picture in my mind of the room and everyone in it, that will forever be etched in my memory.

My father giving Jim mouth to mouth. My sister crying, a look of shock, horror, disbelief on her face. My mom with a small hand towel, fanning it frantically at Jim, trying to do anything to help. I was behind her and couldn't see her face, thank God.

Jim began coughing, spitting, breathing.

They scooped him up, grabbed a blanket and put him in the back of the car. My mom and uncle rode in the back with Jim's limp and still wet body. Danny yelling at my dad, "He's not breathing", dad ran every red light as he sped headlong into the darkness and rain. On the way to the hospital Jim stopped breathing several more times. My mom brought him back every time. My parents spent ten terrifying minutes breathing life back into their son. We all prayed, screamed, cried. My sister and I were left with my aunt to wait for a call from the hospital - it was unbearable not knowing if he was dead or alive.

Dad ran into the hospital, with Jim in his arms, drenched from the rain. He had stopped breathing again. Dad frantic, yelled for help, and continued running down the hallway straight into two visiting doctors from the United States. "My son's not breathing" he said. They immediately began administering oxygen, stabilized him, and for the first time in an hour Jim continued breathing on his own.

The next morning in the hospital Jim finally woke up, confused and more than a little self-conscious that under the thin sheet he was still naked. Released that day, he came home, almost as if nothing had happened, and we finished packing for our vacation.

The little hatchet that had helped save Jim's life went back into its drawer.

In 1978 my family lived in an enormous four story house, atop a hill, overlooking the ocean on the tropical island paradise of Penang, Malaysia. We needed every one of those four floors because in addition to our family of five, for nine months out of the year my mom and dad took care of fifteen teenagers whose missionary parents were scattered across Southeast Asia.

One April night my mom awoke to find my dad across the room, flashlight in hand, going through the drawers of his desk. For a few seconds she laid there trying to figure out exactly what he could be looking for in the middle of the night, until she realized that my father was still lying next to her in bed. The man with the flashlight across the room was a burglar. Somehow she kept her wits about her, and waited until the man left the room, to wake my father.

She told him not to be rash, but off he

went feeling completely violated and more than a little angry. He walked into the hall, took the hatchet from the drawer, and quietly tip-toed through every room, searching for the burglar. After a few minutes he found him, along with his two accomplices, on the grass behind the house below the third story balcony, still rummaging through their loot.

Fuming dad ran inside the house looking for something to throw at them and grabbed the typewriter. My mom stopped him, "No!" she said, "you'll kill them, we're three stories up." He went back to the balcony, hatchet in hand and yelled at them. "Stop – I have a gun." He didn't, Malaysia was almost a police state in the seventies - no one had guns, most of the police didn't even carry them.

The men started to run, my father threw the hatchet still in its sheath. Acting like a boomerang, it curved inward and crashed through the second story window of a bedroom filled with several sleeping teenage boys. Later one of them would recall that he didn't remember waking up, he just realized he was awake, standing next to his bed, surrounded by shards of glass.

The Hatchet was followed in quick succession by a drawer full of tools, threats of gunplay, and several chairs. The men all managed to escape leaving behind quite a mess and a frontpage story complete with pictures in the local paper the next day:

"CLOBBERED: PASTOR GIVES BURGLARS A WALLOPING FROM THE 4th FLOOR."

The hatchet, that turned into a weapon of defense, quietly went back into its drawer.

Twenty-five years later after traveling around the world twice, going to the beaches of the Philippines, taken on countless camping trips throughout the west, and being carried to the bottom of the Grand Canyon, our little hatchet was lost in the desert.

My dad had taken the motor home and three of his grandsons to a favorite spot for rock climbing and target practice. Boys being boys, one of them had put the hatchet down and lost it. Dad was pretty saddened - it had been quite a long journey for him and his little hatchet. He replaced it and life moved on.

About a year later dad took another trip to the desert. This time with my mom and my little family. We decided to stop short of our campsite, partway down the bumpy dirt road so we could be in a good spot to catch some wind in the kites we'd brought for the boys. First they needed to stretch their legs after a long drive so off they went exploring.

As they walked not too far from where we had stopped, Miles, looked down and saw something in the dirt. He picked it up and excitedly ran to show his dad and grandpa. My dad stood in utter amazement. Here in the hands of his six-year-old grandson, was that little hatchet. Somehow, through a year of wind, rain, and other desert rats exploring the area, it found its way home.

It no longer sits in a drawer full of tools. It is mounted, proudly, in my father's office. Below it on the small wooden plaque he has written with a permanent marker: **The axe that saved Jim's life.**

I look at it sometimes when I go to my parent's home and wonder, "Were you really just sitting in the dirt for that year waiting to be found, or were you out on another adventure that we'll never know about?" One might think a strange question to ask of an ordinary hatchet, but I have learned over the past forty-five years that it has been with us, that the life of this particular hatchet has been anything but ordinary.

CALL ME ISAAC

It was a hot October day in Penang, Malaysia. My family, several of the teenagers that lived with us, and our new neighbors the Bogdan's, stood around a huge wooden crate containing our washing machine and dryer. Several months earlier, we had packed them to the brim with clothes and a few treasures we wanted during the four years we'd be away from home.

We couldn't bring much, so everything we did bring was important to us. Most of the things were necessities, clothing and such, some were utilitarian, a cookbook, Chloraseptic spray and Sucrets.

We also had a few of the little things to connect us to the life we'd left behind. Things that could be held in our hand, but were more than physical objects, they were a conduit to family and home. I remember at least once a year I would ask my dad if I could dig through the small cigar box he kept in the bottom of his closet. He always obliged. Inside was his stash of Certs candy, a few dollar bills and some American coins. Pictures of grandparents and cousins, and a couple of Disneyland ticket books. There were no E tickets left of course but nearly all of the A's and a few B's were there, waiting to be taken home someday, so we could ride the carousel in Fantasyland.

We had lived for weeks with what we could carry on the plane, so we were excited to say the least to be reunited with our things. My dad and Mr. Bogdan (Uncle Dan to us kids) pried open the crate and my mom opened the door on the washer - empty. She opened the dryer, empty as well. Somewhere during the 8000-mile trip from Riverside, Ca to our new home someone had opened that crate and taken a good deal of the few possessions we were able to bring with us.

Joy to instant sadness, then all of us desperately trying to remember what we had put in there that we would never see again. Mom remembers an audio tape of my first words, lost forever. Uncle Dan was the first to break the tension, or at least attempt to. He shared a story of a pastor, that went a little like this.

One Sunday morning a pastor stands in front of his congregation, he has a nice house, a new car, much nicer than most of theirs. There have been whispers and grumblings about it from the parishioners, and so he decides it is time to address the issue.

"I've been blessed by God for all of the hard work and sacrifices I've made building this church" he says. "Now some of you are concerned that maybe I'm taking advantage of my position, and seem a little envious of what the Lord has seen fit to bless me with. So, I've decided to give it all back to God."

Making quite a show of it he takes out his wallet, his checkbook, the keys to his house and his new car and declares "God, here is everything you've blessed me with, I'm going to give it all back to you! I will throw it all up into the air. Anything you want you can have, anything you want me to keep, just let it fall to the ground." With bravado that would make Ringling Brothers proud, he throws everything up towards heaven, and nothing...comes...back...down.

My mom doesn't remember Dan telling this story. I hadn't thought much about it either in the past forty years until I overheard my mom telling a freshman MK at a retreat a secret she had kept for four decades. The truth of what my mom had sacrificed, or rather was willing to sacrifice was so much more incredible than any physical possession we could have stuffed into a washing machine.

When my dad and mom decided that they would follow the call, listen to that still small voice and become foreign missionaries eight thousand miles away from everything and everyone they knew, my mother heard another voice. Satan whispered into her ear, "If you go one of your children will die. I'm going to take one of your children from you."

She refused to accept fear and say no to the ministry that God would give to our whole family. She left her own mom, weeping on her front lawn, drove towards the airport and got on a plane with her three young children. She didn't tell any of us about the whisper from Satan for decades and says she never really believed it.

It was on one torturous night, as my father drove, my brother's lifeless body to the hospital, that my mom first thought that Satan would attempt to follow through on his threat. Believe me when I say he tried. My brother was dead or nearly dead on more than one occasion during our time overseas, usually with my sister or I standing by his side.

My brother is still here, perhaps a bit worse for wear, but God never allowed Satan to follow through on that threat. All of those times Jim nearly died, looking back on them now, well I think of them a bit differently. I still see my mom's ashen face, but now I understand so much more of what may have been happening in her heart. She must have been thinking that this was all her fault. That she had followed God's call and it was costing the life of her child.

My mom was Abraham; we, her children were Isaac. God said whom shall I send, and she fearlessly said, "Send me."

My parents have never faltered. Have never questioned why they have given over fifty years of their lives to other people's children. My siblings and I have gone through all the questions and anger that so many missionary kids deal with. Yet we came to realize quite early on that this adventure that was our life was such a gift. It is the miracle that has continued to sustain my family through all the hardships and the trials.

It's not that God wants to take things away from us, but He will. The things we hold onto, that find their way between us and Him are the ones He most desires us to surrender, willingly surrender. God never had any intention of having Abraham kill Isaac. But for Abraham to become who God intended him to be, he had to be willing to offer to God that which he held closest to his heart.

What are you holding onto that the Lord is asking you to sacrifice? Does it seem unfair? Does it seem too much? Give your life completely to God and the life you had before will be gone. The good news is the life God offers you in exchange - though difficult - is worth so much more.

GOD'S GRAVITY

In the 1920's scientist looking at the universe and its cosmic dance of gravity and expansion came up with the amount of matter that would be needed to keep both balanced to allow us to neither expand and be ripped apart, nor collapse on ourselves. Five hydrogen particles per cubic meter of space was the perfect number to keep us here.

As they looked and began crunching the numbers they were thunderstruck. We live on the razors edge, perfectly balanced as if by a force beyond our understanding.

What they found was five hydrogen particles per meter of space.

Go ahead, try again to convince me that there is no God and He didn't create the Universe.

Yes, scientists have, since then, found anti-matter and dark matter which they are trying to understand. They also have been bewildered by the past slow down and then the current speeding up of the expansion from seemingly empty space and a force they cannot understand that they've dubbed dark energy.

I live every day in a peaceful knowledge that passes all understanding that when they "get it" it will again show how balanced we are.

Over and over again science shows a benevolent God. When it feels like there is a dark mysterious energy ripping you apart, remember how God made the universe in perfect balance. His gravity will keep you whole.

SILVER AND GOLD

I stared at it for what seemed like an eternity. I remembered finding this piece of silver at a garage sale years ago, one of many I had rescued over the years. Tarnished and ignored, it had sat in someone's cabinet or drawer and then after what I assumed was a tortuous process they had decided to part with it.

More than likely it only cost me a couple of dollars, still, I took it home and with care and love polished it, hid it away, treasured it. I imagined the grand dinner parties I would someday give, of friends remarking on the beauty of every place setting, each one unique and refined. Of the joy I would have in telling them how little I had actually paid for everything. How I had found this particular piece under a pile of junk on a folding table or that one in a box of someone else's discarded dreams.

I have always loved the idea of an elegant dinner with a few close friends. With just the right food, just the right wine, just the right elegant place settings.

Perhaps I did use this silver tray once, I can't be sure. I ended up after so many years with so many garage sale finds that I stopped polishing each piece, stopped displaying them in my sideboard. Instead I would wrap each one carefully, place it in a plastic container and hope that the oxygen wouldn't get to it, so that when - if, I ever had that party I could simply unwrap everything and not have to spend too much time in preparation, silver polish in hand. My time it seemed was becoming more precious and less.

Now I found myself at a crossroads. Recently widowed, a single mother of three, selling the only house my children had ever known as home. I never had a home myself, I am a nomad by nature and by experience; my home has always been wherever my feet have taken me. Once again I had no idea where the path ahead would lead us; no expectations of what our lives would look like in the future.

For years I had collected things, bits and pieces of a life lived here and there. I had moved so often I finally lost count of how many times I had packed and unpacked, each time dragging with me not only cherished memories but tangible evidence of them as well.

Now, seeing them all together, the souvenirs of a nomadic life only looked like a burden to me. I had my children in my arms and I was beginning to feel that some things needed to be put down so I would be able to hold them well enough, close enough. I stood there looking at what once had appeared to me a fine and precious metal, but now only looked like weighted lead.

I wondered, should I now be the one to place this tarnished treasure into the garage sale pile? I might still use it. I could still picture myself having that dinner party one day when the kids were older, and off on their own. But if I did finally have the time, would I really want to spend it polishing silver?

You see the truth is I do have dinner with friends quite frequently and sometimes the food is spectacular, but more often than not it's a pizza eaten off paper plates, which is more than fine. What I realized in that moment is that my priorities have become such that it's more important for me to have leisurely conversations with friends then spend time washing crystal carafes and polishing silver.

In my youth I had an unrealistic expectation that I could get to a place where the things around me would somehow make me better, by making my life better. I had the notion that I would be a better friend, maybe even a better person if I could live a life touched by elegant things.

So, the silver tray was placed, with a certain amount of joy on the garage sale table next to an old waffle iron and some spatulas. As I laid it down a lightness found me and I realized I have, with age arrived at a resting place, a place where I don't desire silver treasures anymore, in fact it is quite the contrary.

They have come to represent to me all the immaterial objects that I have held onto throughout my life, things that don't anchor me, but actually pull me just below the surface of the water. Now more than ever my time, especially the time I have been given to spend with ones so loved as my children and friends is more precious than silver or gold.

MOTHERING THE FATHERLESS

Father's Day 2017

Six weeks after the death of my husband we celebrated my youngest son Cole's sixth birthday. It was joyful and necessary, but odd. Everything would be odd for the rest of our lives I guessed.

For the first couple of years after Dave passed away, whenever we would be at a party or gathering I could tell who Cole had been talking to, strangers would walk up to me crying. I knew the words they were about to say, so eventually I started saying them first "I see you've met my son Cole, I guess he's told you about his dad."

At six with no guile, he would simply walk up to a stranger and tell them all about his dad and how he had just died. He needed to talk about it, but the adults he encountered couldn't deal with the shock of his forthrightness.

That first Father's Day, less than five months after Dave passed away, the boys and I went to a nursery and bought flowers and a small Maple tree.

Everyone in my family helped us plant a memory garden to "celebrate" Father's Day. Today that tree is twenty-five feet tall and I think of Dave every time I park next to it at my parent's house. I'm not sure if my boys do.

We kept "celebrating" Father's Day for a couple of years. The boys were still in public school and would be given assignments to make presents for Father's Day, the teachers would instruct them to make them for Grandpa instead, but every year these projects were wounds to my kids. Watching them being forced to experience this was torture.

It's not that we don't remember their dad. I talk about him all the time. I want them to remember and know him even though they were so young when he died I wonder if they will truly remember him at all. I thank God for the video tapes we have with him playing with the boys. They know his voice and his laugh, they have "memories" from watching those tapes that they otherwise would not have.

I tell them of the crazy things he did, the stories he told me of his youth. As they got older I started adding the sad stories alongside the happy ones. I want them to know who he was, but I fear they only know him from my perspective and that isn't the entirety of him.

At Dave's memorial service I asked if people would take home the self-addressed stamped envelopes I'd provided to write down their memories of him and send them to us so my boys would get to know him from other people's memories as well as mine.

I didn't get a single one back.

Occasionally we have run into people who have told them a story or two about their dad, but most people don't seem to know how to re act to my children. Perhaps in my children's eyes they face their own sadness. Most of the time I can feel them battling their mixed feelings, not sure how to approach my boys and face the situation.

I have always faced it straight on with honesty and truth. At the beginning that was excruciatingly difficult and painful, but I have grown in strength because I was required to. I have given them what I can OF their father, but it isn't a father. They simply don't have a life with him.

So, after a couple of years we stopped going to the gathering at my parents to celebrate father's day and now we ignore it completely.

For us it only serves as a reminder of

what they do not have, and it's not our style to dwell on the negative. I still bring him up whenever I can, I relay to them stories that they are now able to retell, almost as if he told them the stories himself.

My boys have a father, but they did not grow into the men they are with their father, at least not with him by their side.

When a father dies, everyone says that the mother becomes the father too. I can tell you from experience that a mother is never a father, and cannot stand in for one.

I didn't become a father to my boys, I remembered a father to my boys.

I still hope that someday Dave's friends will take the time to write down or film themselves telling my boys "Dave stories", but I know most simply don't know how to do it.

The first step is courage, the second is honesty. I don't want my children to think their father was anything more or less than he was, that wouldn't serve them or him. I know they don't have a full understanding of their dad and on days like today that makes me cry.

If you were a friend of someone who passed away when their children were young, don't pity them. Don't let your fear of the pain scare you away from them. Believe me when I tell you they live with the pain every day, pretending it's not there doesn't make it go away. If suffered alone it only makes it more intense. Instead talk to them, write to them, tell them who their parent was as you knew them.

You have something many of them will never have, memories. I encourage you to share those memories as if they were borrowed possessions. Think of them as something tangible that you've forgotten about but now need to return.

A human being is a complex creature and everyone who encounters another has a piece of the puzzle that makes up that life. Don't be afraid to share it

THIS LITTLE LIGHT OF MINE

Fire can light your way, warm your home and purify. It can also destroy a forest, burn down your house and turn a good thing to ash.

A match can light a candle or a torch.

Anger is the same. It has its place, even Jesus showed righteous anger. But in a world where we use every hurt, every slight, every little disagreement to become enraged beyond what is appropriate, then use words to enflame others instead of hearing with a heart of compassion and at minimum attempt to accept that someone with a differing view is not an enemy - in that world we will breed only violence.

It is not new; it is not greater than it was. It has always been. From Cain and Able, Isaac and Ishmael, Conservative and Liberal, Christian and Muslim, on and on and on... We find reasons to take injury where none is intended.

We take the pain we feel, of a wound real or imagined, run into a dark corner, lick it, infect it with our own disease, nurture with pride the sickness that spreads throughout the body, then when the fever is running high, we lash out with venom and hate.

The cure is not to avoid being wounded, nature does not exist without wounds and pain. Pain is necessary for the process of growth, and wounds are inevitable if we are to explore ourselves and our world and expand our horizons.

The cure is bandaging the wound with acceptance, love and understanding. We will never stop every mad man who decides to end their life while destroying others.

But with hearing comes understanding. Hearing is only possible with listening while not speaking. Hearing is impossible, when one is screaming.

Every time the finger pointing begins, somewhere in the world, another wound becomes infected by it.

We cannot stop the destructive cycle of nature. Hurricanes, earthquakes and fires will continue to come and ravish humanity wherever we live on this tiny blue planet. But we can stop the cyclical wound for wound, shove for shove, bullet for bullet of our own society.

Strike a match today, but before you do, take a deep breath and ask, with that match, are you about to light a candle or a torch?

LONG WALKS AND COLD SHOWERS

I would make the long walk to the mailbox at least twice a week. The dilapidated house my parents rented for MKM, their ministry to the young adult children of missionaries still in the field, sat in the middle of a once glorious ranch, still dotted with orange, avocado and hundred-year-old oak trees. Each walk to the mailbox down the 300-yard driveway and across the street took a good ten minutes.

Somedays it was simply a nice relaxing walk, listening to the singing birds. But quite often it was made praying that a check would be in the box. If there was indeed a check, the walk back home was light. If there was no check, the bills still unpaid, the walk was uphill, literally and figuratively.

Prayers were said then too. Prayers for help. Prayers for peace. Prayers in thanks because He has always come through. I was only 17, but I had learned early, as the child of missionaries who depend on the financial support of dozens, sometimes hundreds just to keep the ministry going, how to live in a place of peace, to know that the Lord would whisper to those who could help that it was time to do so.

I had sat in pews as my parents shared the story of their ministry to kids like me. I knew exactly what they were talking about and how much having people like them and a house like this had helped other MKs to stay focused on God, decide to become missionaries themselves and more times than I'd know, helped one decide to stay alive. I often wondered if those hearing my family singing and my dad asking "Who will bring the water for the wine" understood as well.

It's not comfortable to be a missionaries kid or pastor's kid and watch your dad ask other people for money. I never got used to it. My sister and brother are better at asking for help. I would usually just fade into the background and pray on my walks to that mailbox. I still pray when I pick up my parent's mail, because they still are here, into their 70's and doing everything they can to help MKs. There are four MKs here right now, spending Easter break at the retreat home.

And so it was that yesterday, waking up so I could rush down the hill to meet with realtors to find a rental for me and my boys that I stood in a freezing cold shower here at MKM praying for help. My boys and I are once again transitioning through MKM on our way to the next chapter of our lives. I am also looking for a job so it's been difficult to find someone to rent to me. I wanted to make sure I looked quite presentable so I jumped into the shower to wash my hair - a very rude awakening.

You see this year MKM has hosted more retreats and MKs than ever. It seems every other week at least a few are here. We're thrilled, but we are also realizing that the kids coming here are the same age as the Microwave (replaced last year), faucets (which make their own music of drip, drip drip), the garbage disposal (removed last month), the dishwasher (replaced last month), the washing machine (ok we've had about 4 of those so they're just babies), the furnace (replaced in January), and the two water heaters - one of which has been dead for seven years. The house needs two water heaters because quite often we have 40 or more kids here on a weekend. Let me tell you when the one remaining water heater runs out of hot water and that cold mountain spring water hits you in the winter, you are awake! I wonder how many kids have taken cold showers? We'll never know, because they would never complain.

So yesterday I went to meet the realtors showing me a few houses for rent while wearing a very fashionable hat. It's perfectly fine, I look pretty good in a hat.

I will soon be living somewhere else and not have to be concerned with taking the occasional cold shower. But as I stood there shivering yesterday, thanking God that I have hot, clean water almost every day, I thought about the MKs coming up for more retreats next month and in the fall.

I don't ask for money, I just fade into the background, and pray on the way to the mailbox. But here I am asking for financial help if you can offer it, repair and cleaning help around the house if you can manage it, and prayer when you remember my parents and all the MKs coming through this house.

Written for the Spring 2016 MKM Newsletter
   www.missionarykidsministries.com
   P.O. Box 9286,
   Cedarpines Park, CA 92322

YOU CAN'T DRIVE THROUGH ZION AFTER DARK

Conventional wisdom says to stick to what you know, certainty. Know where you are headed and plan accordingly. Stay on the road you're comfortable with, the one you've traveled before.

At the end of our summer vacation in 2007 my family was ready to get out of our motor home and be back in our own beds. We had done almost everything we had set out to do, seen more than we had hoped to see, now it was simply a matter of covering the final 800 miles or so that lay between us and home.

The last tourist trap we encountered was Ruby's Inn and believe me a tourist trap it was. My parents drove off to see Bryce Canyon leaving my boys and I behind in "town" so that we could see an honest to goodness rodeo. There were horses and bulls and men in cowboy hats, a fitting end to a trip through what once had been the western frontier.

After the best cowboy had been bucked and the last bull lassoed we wandered through the gift shops and bought our final trinkets, "Take something home from every state" had been the idea from mile one.

So around midnight we climbed into our now all too familiar motor home. We were tired and broke - we were done. We had traveled over 4400 miles since we'd left home three weeks earlier and the sentiment had turned from an excited fascination of what may lay around the next bend, to "Let's just get home already".

My father was driving while I read a book. Lost in my fiction and my iPod I missed the entire conversation he and my mom had been having about whether we should stay on Highway 89, past Route 14, which would take us directly back to Interstate 15, or instead continue on another 30 miles to Route 9. They chose Route 9, it sounded like the more interesting road; it seems there was at least one more thing worth seeing on our way home, Zion National Park.

As with everything on this vacation we had not done any research at all, we just drove headlong into it. No reservations, no specific route, we were taking the roads as they came. This was a first for me and it had worked out incredibly well up to that point, we had even managed to find available campsites at Yellowstone Park for three nights, smack dab in the middle of summer. So, we just continued on with nothing set in stone, feeling quite lucky and carefree.

As we turned off Highway 89 onto Route 9 I saw a warning sign on the side of the road, something about large vehicles. We sped by too fast for me to read it in the dark, but within a mile or so I saw another sign which clearly stated that trucks, motor homes and large vehicles must pull over to the side of the road. I told my dad, and he responded, in typical dad fashion, "Nah, what for?"

"I don't know" I said, "but we should find out."

I assume a warning sign is put up for a reason, my father, being the old school missionary that he is, assumes it's just someone trying to mess with him. My mother and I did convince my dad to slow down and pull over just as we approached the largest and what turned out to be the last of the warning signs.

So, the three of us sat on the shoulder

of Route 9 at one o'clock in the morning, in the middle of "nowhere' Utah, staring at the enormous billboard that towered in front of us:

<u>"All vehicles and trailers 7'10" in width and/or 11'4" in height or larger require an escort. Vehicle escorts are available 8am- 8 pm at a fee of $25."</u>

My father immediately balked at the idea, not only of having to wait until morning to continue on, but of having to pay a fee to travel a road everyone else could apparently travel for free. Reluctantly he got out, found the tape measure and he and I stretched it across the back of our new motorhome, "Eight feet four inches" he announced with gloom, six inches too wide. As he and I stood discussing his brilliant idea that we should "just go for it" we agreed to measure the height as well. I don't know why it would have mattered seeing as we were too wide, but I guess he was thinking.... well honestly

I still don't know what he was thinking.

Dad climbed up the ladder with the tape measure, lowered it to me and as I reached up to grab it I saw a sight that left me speechless. There stretched out before me in astounding brilliance was the Milky Way as bright as I had ever seen it. You just don't get to see that many stars in Los Angeles, not real stars anyway.

I had been so busy worrying about what obstacles might lie unseen on the road in front of us, that I hadn't thought about the fact that it was the middle of July with a new moon and being in the desert, miles from the lights of any town, we were in the perfect place at the perfect time it to get a spectacular view of billions upon billions of stars, something my kids had never seen.

I ran and gathered the kids and my mom, we turned off all the lights on the motor home and stared up into the sky. We stood for several minutes, necks craned gazing up as shooting stars streamed overhead, bats dive-bombed towards us and the hundred billion stars in our galaxy painted the sky white like faint whispers of clouds.

We watched the sky for several minutes more then after much discussion turned around, drove back the way we had come and found ourselves at a small camping area near the turnoff we'd taken an hour before. It was a free campground, apparently put there for wayward souls such as us who hadn't done their research about driving through Zion after dark in oversized vehicles. There was even free Wi-Fi at this tiny nothing campsite in the middle of nowhere America.

The next morning, we set off back down Route 9, paid our fee and after waiting for a few minutes, were escorted by a park ranger like celebrities through a seventy-seven-year-old tunnel, 1.1 miles in length – the longest tunnel on earth when it was completed back in 1930. We found out the escort was necessary for large vehicles because this old two-lane tunnel was carved in an arch and any vehicle over eleven feet tall had to drive down the middle of the road, taking up both narrow lanes to avoid hitting the low ceiling on either side. There was no other way a tall (or wide) vehicle could get through it except to drive down the middle, and you couldn't very well drive down the middle of a one-mile-long tunnel unless you were quite certain no one was coming from the other direction. You had to have an escort to radio ahead and stop oncoming traffic at the other end.

When we came out the other side we were shocked at the scene. Sheer cliffs on every side, dropping down nearly one hundred feet in some places, it was terrifying and beautiful and if we had managed to get through the tunnel at midnight, we never would have seen the scenery of Zion National Park.

If we had planned out our trip and added Zion to it, the scenery would have been just as beautiful and the tunnel would have been just as long, dark and frightening; but we would have missed the most awesome sight of all, a galaxy of a hundred billion stars that God had spread out before us like a blanket.

Sometimes it's the miss-steps we take, forcing us to pull over and take a deep breath that bring us the most incredible experiences of all. When we are required to measure ourselves against the unexpected tunnels in front of us, sometimes we find we won't fit through, at least not in the dark. The road we find ourselves on often looks quite different than what we assumed it would be from its description on a map, and what we find along the paths we choose are often not what we drove down them for in the first place.

An un-researched alternate route might yield bridges that are washed out or tunnels you cannot fit through, but it's roadblocks like that, the ones that force you to the shoulder, that give you the opportunity to take a look around and find the beauty in your surroundings,

surroundings you never would have noticed driving past at 70mph.

It's in those times, when all the signs say STOP, that you might discover the entire reason for the trip. If you'll simply pay attention, pull over and look up, you may see something completely unexpected and grander than what you ever could have planned for yourselves; like a hundred billion stars and if you're lucky, a few falling ones as well.

I'm sure I've already missed wonders in my life as I've traveled along, head down, reading a map I've carefully highlighted with the safest and most efficient route. Sometimes to find the most beautiful things in this world you need to just throw out the map and wing it. Which is what I learned on my summer vacation, all because you can't drive through Zion after dark.

BE THE GOOD

Cole came bounding down the stairs and asked what was happening. "Another shooting" I said as I stood in the kitchen watching the unthinkable happen again, this time in my backyard. "Two shooters, 12 killed."

"When this happens I just think about the good things people do" Cole said. "Everything is in balance. There is positive for every negative."

As I stood watching the aftermath of the December 5, 2015 terrorist attack in San Bernardino unfold on TV, my sister called to tell me her daughter's mother-in-law who worked just across the street was in lockdown. I felt that sick all-too-familiar feeling I'm sadly becoming accustomed to.

I thought about Panera Bread. It's just a mile or so from where the shooting was. Every Wednesday since 2007, someone in my family or a friend has gone to pick up a donation of the nightly leftovers at the San Bernardino Panera Bread restaurant, and then divided and delivered it to various charities who feed the hungry. There are a lot of hungry people in this area. I wondered if this would affect those at Panera Bread and if we would get the donation - so many people depend on it.

This city confuses me. The city went bankrupt in 2013. The county is close behind. It's a hole. It's gross. It's dangerous. My heart breaks for it because there is so much going for it despite all the problems we have. We are "on the way" from LA to beautiful mountains full of ski resorts. The roads to Las Vegas, Palm

Springs, Arizona - anywhere East of LA and south of Colorado comes through here. We have a beautiful international airport that's sits virtually empty. We have beautiful weather. We have creative, intense, passionate people who are committed to seeing the San Bernardino area bloom once again.

Still, as I descend from the mountain that overlooks the city, my heart breaks - every.single.time.

I continued on with my day, put the roast beef in the oven, then off to a small craft sale at a women's Bible study to sell some jewelry my dad and I had made. Then at 3:00 o'clock Dawn called again.

The Panera Bread store was closing for the day. They needed someone there now if we wanted the donation. Half of what they had would go to the victims of the shooting and the first responders, we would get the other half. Could I be there in an hour?

I didn't even think no. I just thought hundreds of people were hoping to have bread on Friday and I can't even imagine what it's like to go to bed hungry. Coles words echoed in my head "For every evil done, remember the good someone does." I could go, I could drop everything and go, straight towards the area I should be running from.

I knew I probably wouldn't be in danger. The police wouldn't let me get too close to any known danger, and truth be told, driving anywhere anytime, especially in Southern California, can be dangerous. Besides, it kind of felt like, if this was in fact terrorism, I'd be flipping them the bird by doing something good instead of hiding in fear.

As I pulled out of the church parking lot I heard on the radio "Shooting at Tippecanoe". Dang! That's the street that Panera Bread is on. I called Dawn and asked her to find out where the second shooting was taking place and I continued driving down the hill.

Looking at the city below I couldn't see anything different from five-thousand-feet up. It was surreal to imagine the horror happening down there - it all looked so peaceful.

Twenty minutes later Dawn called back. The second shooting was close to the Panera Bread store, the employees she had just spoken to were on lock down hiding in the office. I kept driving, now only a few miles away from what appeared to be an active terrorist attack.

As I drove down the freeway I kept listening to the radio, hoping it would all be over before I got there. The exit where the initial shooting had occurred was closed of course, but the next exit, Tippecanoe, was still open. I got off and turned towards the area of the second shooting. No one else was worried it seemed, there were cars and trucks everywhere, and police vehicles from every city within a thirty-mile radius.

I called the Panera store; a young woman answered, surprisingly calm. "We're still under lock down. Please don't come near here," she said.

One block away I pulled into a parking lot and sat. My sister called from work and informed me that she would like it very much if I just left the area.

I assured her I was in no danger but would go to my brother's house a few miles away. I almost went to Redlands to see my niece, as it turns out that is where the shooters lived we found out later.

At 5:02 pm Jessica from Panera Bread called back, "If you're still in the area you can come get the bread now - we have a lot of it."

Four employees were still there when I arrived. The younger ones seemed to be in shock. They loaded the bread into the back of the truck and apologized for my having to wait! I told them to go hug their families and that I had been praying for them and handed them some homemade fudge I'd grabbed as I left the church.

A few minutes after I got home, while finishing the now very well done roast the phone rang, it was the woman from the aid office in the mountains who passes out food every week. "Will you have bread for us on Friday?" she asked hopefully. I laughed out loud and told her I had just gotten back from picking it up from San Bernardino. "Don't risk your life for a little bread, it's not worth it," she exclaimed.

Every time there is a shooting or a terrorist attack, I get sick to my stomach and am left feeling frustrated as it seems there is never anything I can do. This time it was my city that was bleeding, and finally, I could take action. It wasn't anything extraordinary. It wasn't something that saved a life. It was just a band aid placed on a gaping wound. But it was - something.

I saw the evil and answered with a

simple act of love. It was a reaction inspired by my son's words. My son was watching me that day and maybe next time he sees an act of savagery the good he chooses to remember, might just be me.

GRAPES OF DROUGHT

Despite the fact that he didn't speak until he was four, he was a gifted child who seemed destined for greatness; still he was at every turn a disappointment. Often difficult to deal with, often refusing to attend classes his academic career found him lacking in many areas, and so it was after college that he found himself without recommendations, and unable to find a teaching position anywhere. In spite of his formidable intellect, he settled for a job that required almost none of it.

Day in and day out he went to work in an office that offered nothing to him but a stipend that could barely support his young wife and himself. The glorious life he imagined he would have seemed to be derailed before it even began and by the mere age of 26, Albert Einstein was spending his days as a clerk in the office of patents, shuffling through the paperwork of lesser minds.

Yet it was there, in the barren empty land of a menial job, that his potential was unleashed. Absent the pressures and intellectual engagement of a university campus, the garden of his mind, un-watered and fallow, he produced the most inspired ideas of his life.

Einstein's miracle year, where he wrote not one, but four world shattering papers in just four months, would never have occurred if he had been anything less than a complete and utter failure.

Without the barrenness of those early years, without the room for daydreams and thought experiments, perhaps his mind never would have made the radical leaps in physics that altered the path of everyone on earth. What this genius, who was voted Time magazines Man of the Century needed to come up with his paradigm shifting revelations, was drought.

We love stories about the underdog. The kid too small to play football who struggles at every turn just to make the team. The child born into extreme poverty who suffers tragedy after tragedy then picks up a guitar at six and spends the next twenty years trying to get anyone to listen to his music.

The older I get the more I tend to look at these difficulties not just as something to be overcome, but also something to be embraced.

Maybe it's not so much about overcoming the challenge of want that makes these true life heroes great, perhaps the greatness is born within the want itself.

The struggle to claw oneself out of a hole is impressive, but what does the hole have to offer?

Without being in the hole in the first place, there is no need to climb, no need to reach. But what makes a man great is not simply overcoming the struggle, it is what is gleaned in the experiencing of the struggle and the richness of character that comes from it.

Several years ago my family went up to Napa Valley on vacation. Our vacation wasn't about wine, well not the drinking of it anyway. My parents aren't drinkers and neither am I, but we wanted to head north on vacation while avoiding San Francisco. We used to be able to go on vacation to San Francisco in a motorhome, but on what would turn out to be our last trip there in 2008 it was shown to us quite clearly that the people of that foggy city despise motorhomes more than cars.

We actually had a news crew standing on a corner, pointing and laughing at us as we drove through the once friendly city. We left, frustrated, decidedly unhappy and determined never to return.

This time we would make our way around the city and head into wine country instead. I had spent the weeks leading up to our departure searching online, then calling several different vineyards trying to find one where my kids and I could take a family friendly vineyard tour. Every time I would ask if they had tours for kids they would reply in shock "Why in the world would you want to take a child on a tour of a vineyard?" I was in turn shocked by their response.

I don't know why someone else who doesn't drink might want to tour a vineyard, I just know for me it's a combination of many things. The science and art of making wine has always been a fascination. Jesus' first miracle involved wine, in fact a word search for "wine" in the Bible brings up 212 verses, which speak repeatedly of the vine, the fruit, the wine.

Obviously there's a deeper story and in my typical style I was determined to find it. I knew there was a lot to be learned and as a homeschool mom, I wanted my kids to learn about what goes into making wine while standing in a vineyard.

So it was, with great relief that on our last day in Napa Valley I finally found a small vineyard that said they would take my family on a private tour.

We arrived mid-afternoon at the tiny little vineyard, parked the RV in the dusty unpaved lot and walked into the ramshackle building. As we headed out the back door, the owner handed us umbrellas to protect us from the sun beating down on this 103° day. We hiked the short distance to the vines and arrived both sweaty and thirsty.

The vines were twisted and scraggly, and aside from a few leaves barely looked alive. The vintner began telling us all sorts of fascinating things about growing grapes. I'm not sure my melting kids and parents were as excited as I was.

Because we had been in the middle of a seriously long and major drought in California I asked how often they had to water the vines. "Oh no!" the gentleman said emphatically, "We almost never water the vines. You see the roots go deep, very deep and drought makes the best wine."

Grapevine roots run thirty feet down, it is there they can find the water. Only when the roots run that deep is the vine ready to produce grapes of worth. Only then will the fruit have the potential to produce a wine flavorful enough to be worth anything to the vintner. Drought will actually cause the vines roots to go even deeper, creating a better tasting wine. Not all of the vines will survive, but the ones that do will produce extremely rich and flavorful grapes. Wine made from these drought grapes will be some of the best and most sought after wines on earth.

Even in the worst drought vintners will

avoid watering their vines if at all possible, and this is one of the things that makes wine so fascinating to me.

You see the flavor of wine does not come from the flesh of the fruit, the flavor comes from the skin. Wine grapes are tiny compared to table grapes, and the skin-to-fruit ratio is much greater, which means the flavor is richer and more intense. This is exactly what vintners want. A grape vine will naturally try to protect the soft fruit and in drought this is done by increasing the thickness of the flavorful skin.

A stressed vine makes great wine.

When planting anything that produces fruit, common sense would suggest you should plant in good sun, with plenty of water on a good plot of land, with very rich soil. That is not the case for wine. For wine you really need two things, good drainage, this is why vines are found on sloping hillsides, and soil that is actually not very good at all. Planting grapes in nutrient poor soil, stresses the vines triggering them to produce the smaller grapes needed for wine.

Vintners love it when their vines are stressed out, it actually adds depth to the wine when the vine has to struggle to get water. As the plant tries to protect the fruit inside it creates a thicker skin and the wine becomes amazingly flavorful. Plant a grapevine in great soil with plenty of water and you'll have wonderfully juicy grapes, that are almost flavorless.

There are two additional things needed to make a wine, pressure and time. To be made into wine, grapes must be gently broken open. Only when the skin is torn and mixed with the juice of the fruit, is the full flavor revealed. To become what it is meant to be, to fulfill its purpose, it must be broken so it can become something else.

It is only at this point that the vintner has a true idea of the potential of what he has grown, and yet, he still must wait.

Some wines are best drunk soon after they are made. Many require years of stillness, a decade or more of quiet, absorbing the flavor of the barrels, while the vintner waits for the moment that the flavors reach their peak expression.

This wine experience and new depth of knowledge made me realize how much we are like those vines. "By their fruit you will know them" it says in Matthew 7:27. If we have deep roots and can get to water we can survive even when there is a drought. Only through struggling do we become flavorful, full bodied, that is when our potential is realized. The most interesting people on earth invariably have a story of hardship to tell. But it is not escaping the hardship that makes them interesting, it is flavor that they developed because of it.

Once again I find myself in the middle of a tremendous struggle and I hate it. I know what's at the end will be rich and rewarding and I know I'm learning another life lesson that will someday be worth it.

But right now, I just want out, I feel like I've been without water long enough, and I am ready to be drenched.

So, I'm asking myself some questions. Is the soil I'm planted in making it easy to find nourishment? If not, that pain I feel is the struggle to grow deeper roots. If I am to be known by the fruit I bear, I need to somehow find peace within the struggle against drought and within the pressure of a life that feels like it may strangle that life right out of me.

If the world will know me by my fruit, then I want to become something worth savoring.

BITTERSWEET REFRAIN

A tear ran down my face as I hit the 605/210 intersection and passed City of Hope. Memories sweet and bitter flooded into my conscious...

One year ago I was heading into ABC/Disney Prospect Studios for my first day of work nearly seventeen years to the day after my husband had started there. I would only be working there for five months on a temporary job, but it still felt surreal. I was driving to Dave's work, passing the hospital where I told my children they were going to lose their father in a matter of days.

I was remembering the first time I had gone to the studio lot in wonder when my husband began working there in 1998. Finally, a job where we didn't have to worry about where next month's rent was going to come from. Security, a fixed schedule - normality.

We were at Disneyland when Dave got the phone call that he had the job for sure. Three years later he would call me from work as I sat at Disneyland having lunch with my mom and sister Dawn. He called to tell me Dawn was getting the interview for a position in the Music Department.

She worked there on and off for years. Full time, maternity fill-in, then back to part-time in the same department. I would join her for a brief time last summer and every day that I drove onto that lot, I felt a little bit of amazement. Over two decades I'd been driving onto this lot, as a wife, as a sister, as a friend, as a vendor and now as an employee.

When my sister and I started our own company, Take 2 Productions, our first placement was on an ABC show. We got a second placement soon after and within a couple of months we were in negotiations for a contract making all the music of the artists we represented available for their shows.

While I was working there last summer my oldest son would come to visit me for lunch and we'd walk the lot where he grew up. We'd wander down the halls of promo where his dad had worked. Onto the set of Grey's Anatomy and General Hospital when they were dark.

Last month as we left after visiting a friend, I asked Miles what being there was like for him. I had a myriad of emotions, and I couldn't imagine how he felt. His dad would bring him and his brothers to work once or twice a month when he had to work Saturdays and they would run the halls and roll down the ramps, squealing and making too much noise.

"It feels kind of like Disneyland" he said. I was a little confused but he continued, "This lot and Disneyland are consistent. My whole life, those are the only two places that have remained the same."

I turned away so he wouldn't see me trying to hold back the tears.

The next day my sister called me, it was her day off so she hadn't checked her email, but someone called to tell her she needed to go check it immediately. A music supervisor wanted to let her know that he was looking for a song to use in a scene on General Hospital. He was looking at "This Changes Everything", written and performed by her son Chris Ryan, to use as a feature on the yearly Nurses Ball episode - their highest rated show every year. Not only that, he wanted Chris to perform it on the show.

We were stunned and hopeful, Chris had been in serious need of a break. But I guess I've missed some important details in the story, because this lot, this studio, this place and these shows were not only an integral part of my children's lives, but Chris's as well.

Dawn's son Chris had always shown an interest in music, but at about twelve he begged for a guitar for Christmas, Dave and I loaned his parents the money to buy him his first crappy guitar. It came straight out of a cardboard box from Guitar Center.

Chris was one of those kids you worry about when they're twelve. A bit awkward, home-schooled, not interested in anything but Pokémon and video games. There's a very good chance you've had a kid like that in your house - I've had three.

When Chris got that guitar, his whole world changed. He fell asleep practicing it every night. As he started getting better, he began to gain a little confidence. He became someone I actually wanted to hang out with. Dave and I were soon separated, but whenever Chris would see him at family events they would talk about music, and Chris couldn't wait to pick his brain and show him how much better he was getting on that guitar. The first time Chris sang in public, Dave was there. A little upstairs club that served as a church on Sundays. It was the place I decided to have Dave's memorial service, in great part because of that connection.

When Chris was fifteen everything changed - for all of us. There are years you can look back on and almost see a cosmic shift. Fifteen was that for Chris. He was asked to play bass in a hard-core band and tour the US for several weeks. Dawn called me in tears moments after she watched the tour van carrying her son, drive down the street and out of sight.

After that tour Chris started writing songs of his own. Love songs, and surprisingly, they were pretty darn good! Sadly, Chris didn't get the chance to share this new life with Dave. Just months before Chris's "new" life took off, Dave had passed away after a six-week battle with lung cancer.

Chris kept writing and getting better at it. After a few months he had enough songs we thought were good enough for him to record an EP. Another artist Dawn and I worked with recorded it for him. I paid for that record, actually Dave paid for that record with the life insurance we had wisely purchased. I don't even know if Chris knows that.

When the album was done and pressed Dawn called me and told me something Chris had said near the end of recording. "I wish Dave was here to see this."

Part of it was that he wished Dave could help him record it I'm sure. What a joy it would have been for them to work on an album together. But I think a great deal of that statement was Chris being proud of all he had managed to accomplish by sixteen, he really wanted Dave to know how much he had grown and how far his music had taken him.

That first song our little company

placed on an ABC show was a Chris Ryan song. We sent them our entire catalog, of a couple hundred songs, they chose a song Chris had written at fifteen and recorded at sixteen. He had decided to remove his last name and use his middle name for stage, so no one knew he was Dawn's son for several years.

Chris has written a couple dozen songs for the ABC music library. He walked into the office himself at seventeen, when his mom wasn't working there and convinced them to buy some of his songs. He's been heard on GMA, 20/20, General Hospital, The View, What Would You Do, so many more.

Three weeks ago, as Miles and I drove onto the lot, I as Chris's manager and Miles as his photographer, I shook my head in wonderment. No matter where we go, we seem to always end up back here. Chris, Dawn, Miles, Dave and I have been all around the world, we have lived adventurous lives. Yet this is a place we always seem to come back to, as if we are magnetized to it.

It is a little, nearly forgotten studio lot, one hundred and one years old. It is secure. It is fixed. It is consistent.

Of all the memories that I have of this place, I think this newest memory will always be the sweetest. Every time I walk past the plaque honoring the 25th anniversary of "Luke and Laura's Wedding" past the faded General Hospital sign, I will remember getting to watch my nephew stand on a set for the first time, singing a song he wrote, just fifty yards away from where Dave worked for eight years.

I can't imagine we have anything else left to do there. But if you'd asked me in 1998 if I thought, I or Dawn or any of us would ever have lived this many lives on the Prospect Lot I would have laughed at you.

I cannot wait until tomorrow. I will turn on the TV with my kids beside me. We will set the DVR to record ABC and watch Chris being beamed from those enormous

satellites we've walked under a hundred times.

"I have to go and finish this promo, I'll call you later. I've got to hit the satellite at 6:30." Dave Jahnsen
>ABC Prospect Lot
>1998-2006

EARN THIS

My generation has not yet earned the rights we were given freely at birth. We are endowed by our Creator with these rights, yes. But for those of us who have these rights actualized here on earth, are we not required by the very idea of that right, to be willing to sacrifice all we have, to ensure those rights be upheld for the helpless? The "Greatest Generation" earned, by the sacrifice of their comforts and their very lives, the moral right to those rights.

Tom Hanks last scene in Saving Private Ryan displays the ideal. Private Ryan, if looked at as an allegory is the fledgling freedom loving nations of the world, including America. Tom Hanks last breath speaks the words that give the movie it's entire purpose - "Earn this." Not enjoy this life we have given you with our sacrifice, EARN this life we have given you with our sacrifice.

The millions who gave their lives in WWII to ensure those rights for us are watching now. Was their sacrifice in vain?

If we, the free, do not with self-sacrifice of everything, give all that we have, including our very lives, to ensure those rights for others, have we then shown to the bestower that we do not in fact deserve such rights endowed upon us?

Can we accept freedom as simply a birthright? This would make us no better than the nobles of old. No better than the self-righteous religious leader living in splendor while peasants outside the church die of hunger. In fact, I believe it would leave us not much better than the terrorist demanding the allegiance or death of others.

"We hold these truths to be self-evident, that ALL men are created equal, endowed by their Creator with certain Inalienable Rights. That among these are Life, Liberty and the pursuit of Happiness." Are these simply words on a page to us now or do they actually represent something more, something greater?

Does not the concept of "Inalienable" and "All" demand, by its very nature, that we demand it not only for ourselves but for the world as a whole? What is at risk is the very humanity we cling to.

"We cannot win this fight" is the battle cry of the pacifist. It is not only cowardly but narcissistic. By not "getting involved" in a fight, where a clear line of good versus evil had been established and recognized, we have taken our humanity, our endowed human rights and spat them back into the face of the Creator. We are aware of the travesties occurring, therefor we are, as human beings endowed with conscience, by default involved. It is our choice whether to ignore the cries of the victims or come to their aid.

How should America then be destroyed? Fight an unwinnable fight that is righteous and worth dying for? Or let Her die of old age in her comfortable bed, as children are beheaded, women are raped and enslaved, and genocide is allowed to proceed unfettered.

The first is noble and deserving of those inalienable rights, the latter is repugnant. I would prefer we go down, every man, woman, and child in America fighting evil in hand to hand combat, with the words "Lord, we did all we could and gave our lives in sacrifice for justice" on our lips. At least then we might be deserving of those rights.

Two weeks ago I stood in Dodger stadium with over 50,000 people listening to

Paul McCartney sing "Let It Be." A smattering of cell phone lights began to appear, and soon the full moon's glow was paled by the thousands of lights being held up in solidarity, it seemed a refreshing sign of hope. I looked around the stadium and began to cry, I'm crying now as I remember it.

When Paul McCartney wrote those words down in 1968, words spoken to him in a dream by his long dead mother, this country was in chaos. To hear him sing it again, to an American audience so different then we were in 1968, so endowed with freedom and peace while the world around us is on fire, was surreal.

We are a parted, partisan people. Are we close enough to being broken hearted about the atrocities being committed around the world that we can finally find agreement that it must end, even if that means once again putting ourselves and everything we hold dear in harm's way just as our grandparents did? I believe the endowment we have been given is not bestowed without expectation. It is a sacred trust.

"And for the support of this Declaration, with a firm reliance on the protection of divine Providence, we mutually pledge to each other our Lives, our Fortunes and our sacred Honor."
    The Declaration of Independence

If not now, when?
If not here, where?
If not us, who?

America, let us once again, pledge our Lives, our Fortunes and our sacred Honor. Let It Be.

THIS STORM OF LIFE

I have been watching, or rather trying to watch "One Strange Rock" on NatGeo for several weeks. I finally turned on Episode Two a few days ago and was able to watch most of it. The episode is entitled "Storm".

Everything about how our planet became compatible to not just life, but a vast and complex web of life, comes from what seems like random accidents happening to Earth over billions of years.

Just the right chunks of rocks with

the right kinds of elements came together to form the earth. Then a huge, 100-thousand-year period of icy asteroids and comets hitting our planet to form the vast oceans and icy caps. Mars and Venus were hit with these as well, but being just a little too far and a little too close to the sun leaves them barren and dry. Earth, right in the "Goldilocks zone" is left with its water in all three states - solid, liquid and gas, critical for what happens next.

Earth and its sister planet, Theia, spin for millions of years in a cosmic dance, finally succumbing to their gravitational pulls, they slam into each other leaving one large planet, with enough debris spewed into space and orbiting Earth to form a moon, but not just any moon. A moon considerably larger than most planetary moons. This collision also leaves the earth spinning and tilted on its axis, a wonderful 23.5-degree tilt, just enough to give us seasons.

No collision means no tilt, no moon, no spin. No tilt means no seasons. No seasons means no vast plant and animal life. No moon, no tides.

Over and over these accidents, this violence, the seemingly random events not only make life on earth possible, but make earth a place where incredibly diverse life can thrive.

It's remarkable, but I turn it off just short of the end, because I have a dentist appointment.

My boys and I had recently moved into my brother's house. After four years of unsuccessfully looking for work and selling almost everything we owned, including our home, Jim had generously invited us to come stay with him. My oldest two boys into a makeshift bedroom in what had been the living room, me and my youngest son in our motorhome in the driveway. After a month spent packing, moving and settling in, I had tried to go back to the only work I had been able to find in those four years, driving kids around LA. Still not unpacked, but in desperate need of money to buy food, I had been trying for days to get back to driving.

To do this required me to claim rides when they became available on the app at noon, one week prior to the ride. Hundreds of drivers, vying for a few hundred rides on an app that crashed as often as it didn't. For over a year, I'd had a reminder set on my phone for 11:55 AM, to remind me to open the app and claim what I could. For whatever reason it seemed to have stopped working. For two weeks I had missed all the available rides.

On a Monday afternoon I finally realized the reminder had simply disappeared off my phone. I added it back in. Tuesday, no reminder. I set it up again. Wednesday, no reminder. I finally managed to get it working again and on Thursday I claimed a few rides for the next week. I breathed a sigh of relief.

After Jim headed to his room to get ready for bed I found myself alone in the living room. I decided to watch a little TV and settle down for the night.

It all happened so fast.

The telltale sound of metal meeting metal. Ending in a sickening thud. But then an unexpected sound. The screeching of tires. As I headed out the front door, wondering if it was someone I knew, like my son who was headed home, I found myself focused on my own car, sitting alone on the street, it's left front bumper crushed. But whatever had hit it was gone, and then the screeching stopped as I heard the second collision. Metal on cement.

Jim appeared in front of me, opening the door of the car, which was now wedged up on the neighbor's small front wall, the driver revving the engine in a failed attempt to flee. I whipped out my camera and began taking photos. First of Jim trying to get the driver to come out of the car, then of the back license plate. After repeatedly telling the woman to turn off the car, Jim finally reached in and took the keys out of the ignition.

Our neighbor crossed the street just as the woman finally got out, shaken and apologetic, thankfully with no signs of injury.

I told the boys to get a chair, a blanket and a bottle of water so she could sit down. "Are you okay?" I asked her. "I'm fine, I'm just so stressed out, I was on my phone and I don't know what happened I'm sorry."

She called her husband, and at my neighbor's insistence I called 911. I was also shaken and confused, but he looked me in the eyes (it was the first time we had met) and said, with a calm determination "Call 911 now."

As we waited for the responding officers we exchanged insurance information and her husband, who has quickly arrived from their house around the corner, asked me to tell the officers that he was driving. I told him I couldn't and wouldn't do that, then asked quietly "She doesn't have a license?" He shook his head, "No."

After nearly an hour of interviewing the woman the officer came to our front door to tell me what had happened. The woman who was driving on a suspended license found out that day that a close friend had died. She began drinking.

Something terrible happened to her. Her reaction to it was a sad and disheartening response, but one I guess that could be considered understandable. Whatever the reason she got into the car, drunk with phone in hand, cannot be so easily dismissed.

Hours earlier I had parked in the spot on the street closest to the driveway. But because the trashcans were out I decided to back up about five feet to give the trash truck room to access them. If I hadn't done that she would have simply crashed into the back door of my car, not the front bumper, fender and wheel. That five feet was a world of difference, thousands of dollars of difference. I had two years left to pay off my car, financed at zero percent interest, a car purchased when I had a good job and a good credit rating, both things that are now, due to my having been out of work for several years, a distant memory. Getting a loan on a car was now an impossibility for me and looking at the damage, it was clear there was a very real possibility the car would be totaled.

I knew it would be weeks before I could drive again to earn any money. And I found it odd in that moment, that this happened on the first day I was able to book a little work using the car that was now sitting crushed in front of me.

After everyone in the house had talked and talked about what had just happened and gone to bed I once again found myself alone in the living room. Trying not to stress out and not to focus too much on what I would do now, now that the only way I had been able to earn a little money was gone.

I put on the last six minutes of episode Two of One Strange Rock - Storm. The first thing I heard was an astronaut say, summing up the thread of the episode, "This cosmic storm that actually has a violent nature to it, is the reason why we are here, why we are able to live so comfortably on this planet. The significance to me is how something so overwhelmingly beautiful could have come from chaos, violence and collisions. It's just amazing to think about this fine line, this balance between being here, surviving and not."

"The storm has not been our enemy, we're not here in spite of it, we're here because of it." Will Smith concludes.

I sat in tears. Those who say God doesn't bring destruction and chaos into our lives to get us to do what we are meant to do, has not paid much attention to my life.

The woman whose life had just collided with mine made some very poor choices, choices I cannot understand, because the very concept of drinking and driving is anathema to me. Her choice led her to my parked car, backed up enough to be hit in a way to make it undrivable. Her poor choices had revealed mine.

I understood in that moment that God was telling me to stop struggling and do exactly what I know, spiritually at least, that I should do. My flesh said I have to get in that car and leave, to work, because that is the logical thing to do, that is the practical thing, that is the "right" thing to do.

I am trying to live out loud; honest, transparent and true. Sometimes that is easy, like right now, because I really have no other option. God has taken everything else, and it turns out everything else was only tethering me to the dock anyway.

When a massive storm is coming you have two choices. Leave your boat tied to the dock or set it free and hope for the best. I currently have no rope and no dock to tie my boat to, so I'm adrift on the sea and as my brother is fond of saying I just need to "get out of the boat." The only calm in the storm is Jesus, and He's telling me to walk with him in faith, which is all I have left.

In the three weeks leading up to my car being crushed, no less than four people had, unsolicited, given me gifts to make living my life possible.

I'm not including my brother or any other members of my family. It's friends, who have followed thru when they heard the voice of God telling them to do something. Every time this happens, I'm still amazed.

I know what I am supposed to do also, I know from confirmation after confirmation the task to be completed that simply waits in front of me - empty pages to be filled.

A prayerful life has led me to the knowing. A prayerful life is required now for the task of completing it. A prayerful heart is what has sprung from the slow and almost methodical peeling away of what the world tells me I should do, from what I tell myself I should do. Gods plan is my only desire, so I am trying to live it. Placed where I am sure I am needed, even if it is just to plant a seed.

I have prayed for God to tell me what to do. And I had waited for Him to tell me, but all this time I had been looking for Him to show me something that would make logical sense in the world.

He had been saying "not that". He was repeating "No, not that either."

He has been consistent and clear, but my desire to do what the world tells me is right had been between His plan and my actions. When I insist over and over again, on helping God out by doing what the world tells me I should, He says gently no.

I had, out of fear, ignored Him long enough that He had to bring a woman whose life was out of control, to violently collide into mine.

My life is a story. It is beautiful and painful and ugly. To tell it will not only bring back emotions I never want to feel again, it will bring the experience to life within me, and I'm afraid of who I will be in those moments. It's very much like being a method actor, and the woman I was is not a woman I want to inhabit again. She is a victim. She is bruised and broken. At the time of her escape she was barely even alive. The only way I know to tell a story is to relive it and that is exactly what I was facing, standing in the street, looking at my crushed car.

I know to make purpose of the experience of pain we must not only learn from it, we must share it.

And so, I begin, in the midst of the storming sea, I take my first step out of the boat...

PERSPECTIVE

It's very interesting to me, as I watch people react, and often overreact to the words another human being says, how easy it is for us to get it wrong.

Interesting because one person hears the words and imagines that they mean acceptance, progress and a solution crafted out of compassion. Yet another will, upon hearing the very same words, imagine they mean fear and hate.

As I perused some of these contradictory statements in the comment section of a political article, my brain unsuccessfully trying to understand how these people can hear the very same words so differently, I ran across a picture on Facebook. I glanced at it as it passed by, then went back and read the caption on the photo.

"If you only focus on the problem, you may miss the best solution."

I didn't understand. I thought to myself "Okay so it's a cat in a sink. I don't get the big drain at the back though. What is the problem this cat has? That the sink doesn't have water in it because of the big drain...Is that a drain? Wait...cats hate water..."

Seriously, I had no clue what I was looking at. A picture of a cat, sitting in the bottom half of a pet carrier, staring at the door. The top of the carrier was off, but the cat was only focused on the door. But that is not what my brain told me I was looking at. I would have sworn that this cat was sitting in a sink.

So I asked my son "What's up with this?"

As soon as he said "The cat is looking

at the door to the carrier..." I understood.

"Oh, now I see it!" I said.

Remember the visual puzzle teachers gave you around fifth grade. The one that looks like a vase, but is also two faces? It was grade school and they were trying to make a point that they hoped would sink deeply into our brains. We are all individuals and we all see things slightly different. That doesn't make one right and one wrong. Asking someone else to tell you what they see may actually help you find a different perspective, a different answer.

The key though, is we have to listen. Listen as if we have no clue what the other person may say without assumptions. Our preconceived ideas often keep us from understanding what another is trying to say.

We are predisposed towards a particular political and moral viewpoint. In fact, scientist have researched it and written a very interesting book about it called Predisposed: Liberals, Conservatives and the Biology of Political Differences.

So if you thought you could simply make a meme, or write a clever blog to enlighten those who you think disagree with you only because they haven't heard your explanation of how it is and how it should be, well I'm sorry but you would, in pretty much every case, be sorely mistaken. It takes quite a bit to get any human being to adjust their way of thinking. It takes time, new experiences and the hearing of others in a quiet and thoughtful way for any of us to even consider that what we are looking at, may in fact be different than what we originally thought.

About a year ago my sister and I received an email from a colleague, we were both hurt and soon mad because the sender was being such a jerk. When my brother heard us discussing how to respond he asked to read the email. "Why are you mad?" he asked. I pointed to a phrase in the email expecting Jimmy to suddenly be as angry as Dawn and I were.

But instead he did a typical Jim thing, he started laughing at us. "That's not what he's saying" Jim insisted, "he didn't say that."

"Well of course he did" I argued, "right there."

Jim then read the email out loud, with inflections and tone, not of someone saying what Dawn and I had both heard, but of something completely different, complimentary in fact.

"Oh," I said, "Oh my gosh!"

Then Jim said something that I still think about nearly every day. "You assume the negative. You are hearing negative things that you think other people are saying about you. Why do you do that?"

Because we all do that to some degree. We all walk into a room and assume everyone else in the room is judging us somehow, because we are judging ourselves. But if we can just stop for a minute and imagine that everyone else has the same fears and insecurities we carry, perhaps we can let our guard down a bit, stop focusing on the negative things we assume someone is saying and finally hear each other.

Something in my brain told me that I was looking at a picture of a cat in a sink. Does that make me stupid? Well NOW I know that it's obviously a cat in the bottom of a pet carrier. Am I smarter because I know that? Not really. But I am now able to see this picture from a different perspective, only because I swallowed my pride and asked my son to explain to me what he saw.

Perhaps that ignorant, awful, hate filled friend you have that obviously despises you and everything you believe in actually doesn't. Maybe, just maybe they see a vase and not two faces.

Or maybe, they see a cat in a sink.

CHOOSE HOPE

Each and every day there is a choice between fear and hope. I make the choice and it is not a lie. I choose the smallest part of me, the tiny truth that I am still sure of and I speak it as if it is burning like a raging inferno.

But there are moments when it is not a flame or even a spark, but only an ember barely aglow.

Yet, I still choose hope. I reject the loudest voice demanding to be heard. The one that is fear, the one that is regret, that is screaming as if in terror. It is not denial, it is instead a decision, a choice.

Every day is a struggle between these two voices and every day one wins. It would be easy to simply listen to the loudest voice. But fear almost always seems louder than hope, because fear is primal and hope is spiritual.

Once more today I choose to still myself at the rising of the sun. To deny fear it's voice and listen instead to the quiet whisper of hope.

It is not a lie; it is a choice.

EPILOUGE
An Introduction to
"Before I Was a Butterfly"

For the first time in my life I froze in fear, not knowing what to do, but knowing for sure I should not run or speak. I looked into his eyes and my mind raced, desperately trying to figure out what was happening. I had no recognition of the person standing in front of me, the person I had married just seven days earlier.

The eyes were dead and cold, accusatory and angry. The kind of anger one imagines happens to a person just before they break with reality and turn violent.

Confusion and fear battled in my head, as I tried to understand what in the world had just happened to cause the man I had married days earlier to disappear, only to have this creature inhabit his body.

I waited for him, now standing inches from my face, yelling, degrading turning red with anger, to hit me. I knew it was coming, I was preparing myself for the pain. But it didn't happen, instead he just continued to yell.

I finally averted my eyes from his and looked to the ground. I stopped trying to justify the actions that had set him off, my purchasing twenty dollars worth of plants for our new apartment, and I apologized. I knew I hadn't committed any actual offense, especially one worthy of this treatment, but in the back of my brain something told me to give him what he wanted, to some-how, anyhow defuse the volatile situation so I could get out of it. I said, "I'm sorry" and looked down in submission, as the air reentered the room.

Look for Beth's new book
"Before I Was A Butterfly" coming soon.

About the Author

Beth is the child of missionaries and spent her formative years living in several states as well as Malaysia and The Philippines. She has worked in the music industry since she was sixteen, and with her company Take 2 Productions has been an executive producer, concert promoter, and managed the Christian hardcore band Sleeping Giant.

She wrote the forward to the book God's Not Dead (And Neither Are We) by Jerry Wilson.

Of Joy and Sorrow is her literary debut. She is currently working on her second non-fiction book entitled 'Before I Was A Butterfly', about her emotionally abusive marriage, and suddenly becoming a widow and a single mother of three young children at just thirty-eight years old.

She lives in Southern California with her brother and her three boys.

Send inquiries regarding information,
book club/group orders,
or speaking engagements to
Beth@BethJahnsen.com
Subject line: Of Joy And Sorrow

Of Joy and Sorrow
By Beth Wisner Jahnsen
Is available for purchase on
Amazon.com
and at BethJahnsen.com

Made in the USA
Middletown, DE
05 February 2019